Words of Life

THE BIBLE DAY BY DAY

SEPTEMBER–DECEMBER 2007

HODDER

Copyright © 2007 by The Salvation Army
International Headquarters, 101 Queen Victoria Street,
London EC4P 4EP, UK

First published in Great Britain in 2007

1

British Library Cataloguing in Publication Data
A record for this book is available from the British Library

ISBN: 978 0340 910382

Printed in the UK by CPI Bookmarque,
Croydon, CR0 4TD

Hodder & Stoughton
A Division of Hodder Headline Ltd
338 Euston Road
London NW1 3BH, UK
www.hodderchristianbooks.co.uk

Contents

SUNDAYS

In line with the custom of *Words of Life* to treat Sunday readings differently from those for the other days of the week, most of the Sunday readings in this edition feature songs and prayer-poems by the author, in which brevity and poetry combine powerfully to crystallise great truths in a few words.

From the Writer of *Words of Life* . . .

P erhaps it's my age, but words don't come as rapidly to my tongue as they used to. They are as quick as ever to my mind, but transferring them to my tongue is another matter. I have to give them time, coach them for a while, allow them to revise themselves! But I shouldn't grumble too much. I can still read, hear, write and speak words, and each one is precious.

Let me suggest that when you turn to your Bible, you take it gently and gratefully into your hands and, before you ask anything of it, thank God for it. Our God in Christ remembers the magnificence of words from the days when he walked the highways and byways of Palestine. And when Jesus returned to be with the Father, God did not stop speaking to us! Through the Holy Spirit he still uses words to communicate with us . . . if we let him. Not least through the Bible, which not for nothing we call the Word.

So, let's allow God to speak to us through Scripture – including its silences, for sometimes Jesus explains his teaching only in part. His plan, it seems, is for us sometimes to work out for ourselves the truth he imparts – by his living, as well as his speaking. John 1:1 declares: 'The Word was God.' We make no error, I believe, when we say also, 'The Word is God.'

> God came to earth on one dark night;
> Nothing to see but scattered light.
> Silence had fallen, crashed in joy,
> Over the birthplace of one small boy.
>
> He said a Word and that sufficed;
> He was the Word and Love was Christ!
>   *John Gowans*
>   *General (Retired)*

Abbreviations

JBP	*The New Testament in Modern English*, J. B. Phillips, Geoffrey Bles, 1958.
KJV	King James Bible (Authorised Version)
NEB	New English Bible
NIV	New International Version

Applause, Applause

Introduction

There is no doubt about the sensitive insight of Jesus of Nazareth. He had a discernment of situations and noted potential. When a sick woman touched his garments in a crowd he knew that virtue, power, had reached her from him (Luke 8:43–48).

'He knew what was in a man' (John 2:25). He knew, for instance, that we all respond to approval like children do. If we do something right or something beautiful, we are pleased when it is noticed – and that isn't a bad thing provided we don't become too proud of ourselves!

The most interesting part of our subject now is to discover that the praise freely given by Jesus was given to unlikely people! Let's examine the width of his charity and how loud his applause. And perhaps discover how and when to give our praise and thanks to others.

> We always hide
> The way we feel
> Until it's far too late.
> We secretly
> Admire someone,
> But stupidly we wait
> Till death has put a world between
> Their eyes and ears and ours;
> And only when they've gone
> We find
> That we have speaking powers!
> O help us, Lord,
> To say our thanks,
> Express our love somehow,
> And quite without embarrassment
> To give the flowers
> Now!

Because You Say So

....

'Simon answered, "Master, we've worked hard all night and haven't caught anything. But because you say so, I will let down the nets"' (v. 5).

Simon Peter was not a beginner in the art of catching fish and surely would not normally have considered letting down his nets again at this point. His long experience told him there would be little chance of success following failure. Every fisherman's optimism has a limit and Peter had reached his. His companions no doubt shared his realistic pessimism. However . . .

John described himself as 'the disciple whom Jesus loved' (John 13:23). Peter was certainly also much loved by Jesus, but he seems to have been a different sort of follower. There was a lot about him that Jesus applauded. The Master must have laughed at this likable disciple who could walk on water when he told him to do so (see Matthew 14:28–29) – even if only briefly! Now Peter is saying, 'We've worked hard all night and haven't caught anything. But because you say so, I will let down the nets.'

Peter's simple obedience was rewarded with a success he never knew before. Two boats overflowing with fish were proof of the Master's affection for his followers. And Jesus added a promise for Peter: '"Don't be afraid; from now on you will catch men"' (Luke 5:10).

Most Christians know that 'worked all night and caught nothing' feeling. I certainly do! I have tried to minister, to counsel, to comfort a person many times, thinking nothing would ever come of it. My efforts seemed useless. Then I have tried just one more time, perhaps in the simplicity of a conversation over a kitchen table, because my Christ said I should. And beautiful things have happened. My 'boat' has been filled with joy to the point of sinking.

At such times I have joined with Peter on his knees, unworthy of the privilege which had been mine. 'Go away from me, Lord; I am a sinful man!' (v. 8). Who deserves such a priceless partnership with Jesus?

....

To ponder:
'When we have exhausted our store of endurance . . . our Father's full giving is only begun.'

Annie Johnson Flint

2

They Left Everything

*'Jesus said to Simon, "Don't be afraid; from now on you
will be catching men." So they pulled their boats up on shore,
left everything and followed him' (vv. 10, 11).*

Staggering words: 'They left everything.' Their job. Their ambitions.
Their freedom. I've watched Christians at work in many countries
and have come to believe that the better Christians are those who
choose to lose! I've also noticed that any spiritual growth in me can be
traced to my willingness to let go of something or other in accordance
with the patient guidance of God.

Faced with the Choice

Faced with the choice, I'll choose your way not mine;
All voices silent but the voice divine;
The plans I've planned surrender at your call,
With your designs I will displace my all,
My will renounce, my lawful rights refuse.
Faced with the choice, with joy, your way I'll choose.
Though far from faultless, take the best I offer;
This living gift of 'me' accept to use.
Faced with the choice, I turn from my ambitions,
Your will for me with peace of heart I'll choose.
Called to your service, this alone I ask:
Lord, make your servant equal for the task.

Exquisite Blessing!

'"Rejoice in that day and leap for joy, because great is your reward in heaven. For that is how their fathers treated the prophets"' (v. 23).

When Scripture records that Jesus looked at his disciples before he spoke, we can be sure that what he was about to say was of great importance and intended especially for his followers. This time his message was one of great encouragement. We have become so accustomed to the word 'blessed' that sometimes we fail to grasp its full significance. Perhaps we should add an exclamation mark after it, or expand it to say something like: 'You will receive exquisite blessing!'

In this short passage the word is used that way five times: the poor will become exquisitely rich; the hungry will be extravagantly fed; those who weep will be deeply comforted; the marginalised will be magnificently honoured; the 'nobodies' in the eyes of the world will be welcomed into the fellowship of the prophets of God and they will jump for joy!

Just as the Master looked into the eyes of his disciples of yesteryear so he looks into ours, his disciples of today. But rather than inflating our egos, that should call forth from us feelings of deep humility.

I give my age away when I recall the Salvation Army 'star card' which recorded a child's attendance at Sunday school. At the end of the year mine usually stated that I had received full marks, but honesty demands that marks should sometimes have been deducted for lateness or less than ideal behaviour.

I was not perfect then, and I'm not perfect today. But just as the Master was well aware of his disciples' imperfections yet blessed them anyway, so he blesses and uses me. Yes, even me – and you!

To ponder:
The Christian doctrine of perfection can be said to rest on the words of Jesus: 'Be perfect, therefore, as your heavenly Father is perfect' (Matthew 5:48). Luke's Gospel (6:36) has it: 'Be merciful, just as your Father is merciful.' What's in a word?

Ungrateful and Wicked?

'"Lend to them without expecting to get anything back. Then your reward will be great, and you will be sons of the Most High, because he is kind to the ungrateful and wicked"' (v. 35).

The Bible speaks of the tears and unhappiness of Jesus. But I think he smiled often too. Even when he spoke about the ungrateful and the wicked I believe he often had a loving look in his eyes. How are we to recognise these unattractive people? Some are well disguised. They don't wear lapel badges like members of Rotary. How convenient if they did! It would save us from the mistake of trusting the wrong people. Except Jesus tells us to risk doing just that. And promises that if we offer compassion without seeking a reward we can be sure of receiving one!

Such selflessness is not only approved by Christ but modelled by him as well. The message of Jesus is crystal clear. We are invited to show exceptional kindness to those who don't deserve it: those who are unattractive; those who are unlikely to repay our generosity.

Christians are meant to be unusual, even extravagant in their compassion. Jesus spelled it out for us: '"If you love those who love you, what credit is that to you? . . . And if you do good to those who are good to you, what credit is that to you? . . . love your enemies, do good to them"' (vv. 32, 33, 35).

As we might expect, the reward mentioned by the Christ is a spiritual one – and a staggering one. 'Your reward will be great, and you will be sons of the Most High, because he is kind to the ungrateful and wicked' (v. 35). Our task is not easy but we have signed on to love the unlovable as we love our best friends. We should expect a few gasps from unbelievers!

Could you love the unloved, never reckoning the cost,
Giving them comfort and care?
Could you seek the unloved, in the legion of the lost,
Sharing their grief and despair?

Meredith Wilson

The Wise are Advised

* *

' "I will show you what he is like who comes to me and hears my words and puts them into practice. He is like a man building a house, who dug down deep and laid the foundation on rock" ' (v. 47, 48).

It's been suggested that in this passage Jesus is talking about himself as the Rock of Ages. It's certainly true that he is the unmoving Rock upon which we can rely but he is surely referring here to the wise people who not only listen to his teaching but also put it into practice.

Obedience is the unshakable, safe position we should choose. We are foolish to disobey Christ's commands but he will not force us to be obedient against our will.

Listen to the sobs of the Saviour as he heads for Jerusalem and his crucifixion: '"O Jerusalem . . . I have longed to gather your children together . . . but you were not willing! Look, your house is left to you desolate"' (Luke 13:34, 35).

The brightest of us are fools if we ignore his guidance. But if we're honest we must all confess to times of disobedience and stupidity. I would have to be the first. When we refuse to practise the wisdom Christ shares with us we hurt ourselves, reduce our usefulness, make ourselves ugly in spirit. When we are foolish we choose to make ourselves less than we are. Who knowingly would do that? Crazy!

The most terrible question ever asked by Jesus is found in Luke 6:46: '"Why do you call me, 'Lord, Lord,' and do not do what I say?"' Is it too much of a simplification to suggest that many of the Church's weaknesses arise from the reluctance of members to apply the teaching of Jesus rigorously?

Jesus tells us the wise go to him, hear his words and put them into practice (v. 47). The practice bit is the hardest. It's all about obedience. Personal application of everything Jesus suggests is vital. And total obedience is perfect worship.

* *

To ponder:
'On Christ, the solid rock, I stand. All other ground is sinking sand.'

Edward Mote

Amazement and Admiration

∙∙∙

'When Jesus heard this, he was amazed at him, and turning to the crowd following him, he said, "I tell you, I have not found such great faith even in Israel"' (v. 9).

Centurions get a pretty good press in the New Testament. The centurion who witnessed the crucifixion of Christ is reported in a positive light: 'The centurion, seeing what had happened, praised God and said, "Surely this was a righteous man"' (Luke 23:47). Another centurion – Cornelius, of the Italian Regiment – was privileged to receive angelic instructions. He and all his family were God-fearing, gave generously to people in need and prayed to God regularly. The details are in Acts 10.

But the centurion in Capernaum gets the prize for faith. Luke's account of the humility of the centurion and his deference towards Jesus leads us, too, to admire this Roman. He did not feel he could convey his wish directly to the Master. He felt he did not deserve the right to trouble Jesus by receiving him in his house.

And the centurion's confidence in the ability of the Healer to work miracles from a distance particularly touches us, as it did the Christ. The *NIV* translation speaks of the amazement of Jesus, and the *NEB* talks of Jesus' admiration for the centurion. The fact that the owner of a mere slave was ready to go to such lengths for the slave's welfare moved the heart of the Son of Man. It staggered him that a man not of his nation did not doubt for a moment the ability of Jesus to bring healing. Jesus applauded the attitude of an 'outsider'. The applause was deserved.

What does this example of total faith have to say to us? Firstly, we admire it as Jesus did. Secondly, we are shamed by our own sometimes fragile and uncertain faith. Thirdly, we need to ask regularly for a stronger faith in the Son of God and exercise it as often as we can.

∙∙∙

To ponder:
Believing and trusting are kinds of worship.

A Positive Influence

'"Blessed is the man who does not fall away on account of me"' (v. 23).

John the Baptist was nothing if not a man of strong conviction. From the beginning this prophet recognised Jesus as 'the Lamb of God', the One who would baptise with the Holy Spirit, the messenger who would become more prominent than himself. All the Gospels comment on John, one of the most helpful accounts of him being found in John 1:15–34.

In Luke 7 we find a moment of doubt and discouragement in the mind of the prophet. Perhaps the uncertainty came from John's followers rather than himself, but it was in John's name that Jesus was asked by a group of John's followers: 'Are you the one who was to come, or should we expect someone else?'

Jesus was sensitive to the man of God and his questioning. His answer was that the questioners should go back to John and report what they had seen and heard: ' "The blind receive sight, the lame walk, those who have leprosy are cured, the deaf hear, the dead are raised, and the good news is preached to the poor"' (v. 22). That should be evidence enough and Jesus' additional praise of John must have comforted him: 'A prophet? Yes, I tell you, and more than a prophet' (v. 26).

I wonder if there was a tremble in the voice of Jesus when he said, ' "Blessed is the man who does not fall away on account of me"' (v. 23). He knew John's impact for good was precious and must not be eroded by others. The message of this encounter is plain. Every Christian has an influence for good on those he or she interacts with. None of us must be 'a stumbling-block' (v. 23, *NEB*) to others.

Seeds now we are sowing, each day that we live,
That must to our future its character give;
When God sends his reapers, our gladness or woe
Will spring from the nature of seeds we now sow.
Richard Slater

Acceptable Extravagance?

* * *

*'"Do you see this woman? I came into your house. You did not give me
any water for my feet, but she wet my feet with her tears and wiped
them with her hair. You did not give me a kiss, but this woman, from
the time I entered, has not stopped kissing my feet. You did not put oil
on my head, but she has poured perfume on my feet"' (vv. 44–46).*

Some other rabbis would not even look at a woman. They would
rather close their eyes and risk walking into obstacles! Some rabbis
would never talk with a woman let alone receive a gift or accept a kiss
from her. Certainly no rabbi would associate with a woman 'who had
lived a sinful life in that town' (v. 37). She must have gatecrashed the
Pharisee's party at which Jesus was a guest. She would never have
been on the invited list. Her behaviour was totally unacceptable to the
host but Jesus was not disturbed by it. In fact he took pains to make
clear his approval of her.

Those who know something of the new life that comes from spiritual
cleansing, forgiveness from sin, understand that exaggerated response
and overwhelming thanksgiving are normal. Gratitude is a kind of love
and has to be expressed, sometimes enthusiastically. Jesus said:
'Therefore, I tell you, her many sins have been forgiven – for she loved
much. But he who has been forgiven little, loves little' (v. 47).

If some of us are by nature reticent in expressing our feelings in any
dramatic way, we should not feel guilty about it. We might not go in for
dancing, washing feet with tears, pouring out expensive perfume,
kissing and hugging, but we will find other ways of sharing our
happiness. Jesus said: 'Your faith has saved you; go in peace' (v. 50). We
can do that quietly if we like!

* * *

> Love has a language, all its own making,
> Voiced in its giving, love gives its best;
> Instant and constant with joy while awaking,
> Tells its own story – love stands the test.
> *Joseph Buck*

Home-made Excuses!

'"A certain man was preparing a great banquet and invited many guests. At the time of the banquet he sent his servant to tell those who had been invited, 'Come, for everything is now ready.' But they all alike began to make excuses"' (vv. 16-18).

In this parable we see the danger of missing the experience of a lifetime through being busy with secondary matters. We Christians should have our priorities in the right order but most of us know what it's like to make an excuse which we've regretted afterwards.

Expensive Excuses!

I've made a few excuses
In my time.
And I'm ashamed about it,
They're all mine.
When asked to counsel someone
In dismay.
I'd let some petty thing get
In my way.
I could have changed the date and
Not refused.
I didn't want to do that,
So excused!
Excuses, Lord, have no place
In your style.
Help me to do my duties
With a smile!

From Your Own Pocket?

'These women were helping to support them out of their own means' (v. 3).

The writer of the Gospel of Luke takes the trouble to bring this little picture to our eyes, for several reasons, I think. The event shows us something of the life of Jesus when he was travelling the countryside. The effort of walking from town to village and village to city must have exhausted the strength of the healthiest among the disciples and others accompanying them. There were no certain lodgings and the loan of a donkey for transport was a rare exception. When Jesus said he had nowhere to lay his head this was often the plain truth. Such hospitality as he received was dependent upon his popularity as a teacher and the capacity of the public to be generous.

Clearly a colourful group of people sometimes accompanied the Christ on his travels. They included people who had been healed by him. Some had been possessed by evil spirits, others had suffered from disease.

Several notable women were among them, putting the lie to the notion held by some that the women friends of Jesus were all nobodies. We have a mixed lot here. One earns personal mention: 'Joanna the wife of Chuza, the manager of Herod's household' (v. 3).

Was the writer thinking of the incident of the feeding of the five thousand when Jesus said his disciples should look after the problem from their own resources? Gifts are relative things. That which is sacrifice to one is nothing of significance to another. The willingness of these women to find a solution to a challenging situation out of their own purses must have pleased Jesus considerably.

To ponder:
'Teach us, good Lord, to serve thee as thou deservest: to give, and not to count the cost; to fight, and not to heed the wounds; to toil, and not to seek for rest; to labour, and not to ask for any reward save that of knowing that we do thy will.'

Ignatius of Loyola

Stay Right There

'The man from whom the demons had gone out begged to go with him, but Jesus sent him away, saying, "Return home and tell how much God has done for you." So the man went away and told all over the town how much Jesus had done for him' (vv. 38, 39).

It's a good thing most Christians have taken seriously the words of Jesus: '"Go and make disciples of all nations . . . teaching them to obey everything I have commanded you"' (Matthew 28:19, 20). Since it was born, the Church of Christ has been international in its interests.

The Salvation Army had hardly 'opened fire' in the East End of London before it was publishing a passionate magazine with the title *All the World*, even though the movement was at that time operating in only three or four countries. That act of faith was not over-optimism – The Salvation Army is now at work in 111 countries.

In this Bible passage the man who was dramatically healed wished immediately to join his Saviour's energetic team. He may have been surprised at the reaction. His offer was accepted but his field of service was to be confined to his home town. Charity can begin at home? One can be as called to stay as one is called to go!

Forty-five years ago I was appointed resident pastor and leading evangelist to a modest-sized Salvation Army congregation in Essex, England. Along with my wife, I became anyone's servant in the town. One of the 'elders' of the congregation was called John, as I am. He was about my own age and became my friend, which he still is. He was not perfect of course, as I am not. But his influence on the congregation, on his family, on the congregation's funding of overseas projects, on Christian stewardship, was staggering. And his influence on me was equally good!

I subsequently wandered the world in Salvation Army mission appointments. The other John never left Essex. Many people are glad he stayed and served the Lord faithfully just where he was.

To ponder:
Across the sea, or across the street. When God calls, we must go.

Two Knew!

' "Who touched me?" Jesus asked. When they all denied it,
Peter said, "Master, the people are crowding and pressing against you."
But Jesus said, "Someone touched me; I know that power has
gone out from me" ' (vv. 45, 46).

Jesus approved of this woman for various reasons. For a start he must have liked her courage, which was well beyond the ordinary. Many in the crowd around her believed her twelve-year-long haemorrhage was punishment for weakness or wickedness. From a ceremonial, religious point of view her illness made her unclean. Any other rabbi would certainly have kept his distance. But not Jesus.

The woman had suffered this double burden – the illness and its religious consequence – for twelve years but she had not given up her hope of liberation. Luke – himself a doctor – tells us, 'No-one could heal her' (v. 43) and Mark, in his Gospel account, does nothing to spare Luke's profession: 'She had suffered a great deal under the care of many doctors and had spent all she had, yet instead of getting better she grew worse' (Mark 5:26).

'If I just touch his clothes, I will be healed,' said the woman (Mark 5:28). She would not risk contaminating him ceremonially by touching his person, not even to gain healing, but she believed that touching his garment would suffice. What faith!

We're told the crowds were almost crushing him but Jesus knew something wonderful had taken place. No one else knew it, but he and she knew! I'm not much of a saint but more than once I've been in a place of worship when I've had the nerve to reach out to Jesus and have received the inspiration, healing, correction, forgiveness, comfort I desperately needed without anyone else being aware of the special nature of the moment.

But on each of those occasions two people knew what had happened. Jesus let virtue travel out of him and its beauty was unforgettably received by an undeserving me. Praise God!

To ponder:
How close are we to Jesus? Touching distance?

13

Admiring the Admirable

'"What about you?" he asked. "Who do you say I am?"
Peter answered, "The Christ of God"' (v. 20).

As well as the 'bouquets' there were also 'brickbats' handed out by Jesus. But we mustn't for a moment think he saw only the negative in situations or the hopelessness of the fragile people around him. While, like every good teacher, he did not withhold correction or ignore people's mistakes he also seized every opportunity to encourage his team members and applaud their successes.

The good and bad of Simon Peter were equally visible. In today's passage Simon blurts out the truth which had dawned on him: Jesus is 'The Christ of God' (v. 20). In Matthew's account of this incident (16:13–19) Jesus recognises Simon's spiritual awareness and calls him blessed (v. 17). What an encouragement for Simon when Jesus tells him: '"I tell you that you are Peter, and on this rock I will build my church"' (v. 18)!

But soon after this, after Jesus had spoken to his disciples about his coming death, Peter's rash words – '"Never, Lord! This shall never happen to you!"' (Matthew 16:22) – bring swift correction. The disciple must have been cut to the quick by his Master's response: '"Get behind me, Satan! You are a stumbling-block to me; you do not have in mind the things of God"' (v. 23). For a moment the 'rock' must have felt like an insignificant pebble.

We should learn from this. Let's take comfort in the encouragement God so often sends our way, usually through the words of other people. Let's also accept divine reproof when we realise we have failed the Lord we follow. That reproof will have been spoken in love.

> The broken heart the Lord will favour,
> The contrite spirit he will bless;
> He came to be the lost one's Saviour,
> He came to be the sinner's friend.
> *Richard Slater*

Who Matters Most?

....

'Jesus, knowing their thoughts, took a little child and made him stand beside him. Then he said to them, "Whoever welcomes this little child in my name welcomes me" ' (vv. 47, 48).

In the opinion of Christ, children have immense importance and when we make room for the little ones we can depend on his support. Why does he think they matter most? Perhaps because there is hope for children. There's not much hope for some of their elders, who demonstrate no flexibility in their thought.

It's worth our while teaching a child that sharing is beautiful, that honesty is for everyone's good, that thoughtful manners are attractive and that through these things they can become contributors to a better world. We want them to understand that bullying is repulsive, that dirty language is never clever or amusing, that selfishness is not admirable. When we help children cultivate wholesomeness, healthiness and – why not – holiness it is not an exercise in robotics, nor in attempting to perpetuate Victorian standards, it is helping the children to be the best they can be.

I'm not saying that when an older person has become greedy, miserly or self-centred we should abandon them! The possibility of revolutionary change does not end at sixty, or any other age. But children generally have many more years ahead of them than their elders. Focusing on them is an investment in all our futures.

Children are also reminders to us of innocence and unselfconsciousness. Although children are not perfect, we see humility of the best kind among them. Jesus once asked his disciples what they were talking about. There was a long silence. They had been discussing which of them was the greatest. Indicating a child who was standing with them, Jesus said, ' "He who is least among you all – he is the greatest" ' (v. 48).

....

To ponder:
Have we grown wiser as well as older? What have we gained – and lost – as the years have passed?

Not One of Us?

∙∙∙

'"We tried to stop him, because he is not one of us." "Do not stop him,"
Jesus said, "for whoever is not against you is for you"' (vv. 49, 50).

I was to lead a Sunday morning service in California and was gently
told that the singing might be something of a challenge. They had
not had a pianist or organist for some time. I sympathised and suggested a volunteer musician to fill the gap might be found by making
an announcement of our need in a local newspaper. I was then told
this had been tried without success. Only one person responded. She
would be glad to help, she said, but confessed she was 'not much of a
Christian'.

Her offer was turned down. 'She was not really our kind,' I was told.
I didn't know whether to laugh or cry. Christ would have told them to
recognise angels when they are sent to them: '"Whoever is not against
you is for you"' (v. 50).

It is prissy at least, and possibly blasphemous, to talk as if only the
spotless and impeccable can be any use to God Almighty and his
Church. Mark's Gospel adds more information on what Jesus actually
said on this occasion: '"No-one who does a miracle in my name can in
the next moment say anything bad about me, for whoever is not
against us is for us. I tell you the truth, anyone who gives you a cup of
water in my name because you belong to Christ will certainly not lose
his reward"' (9:39–41).

In the service of Jesus . . .

> *You don't have to be clever, though it may well help,*
> *You don't have to be handsome, praise God!*
> *You don't have to be wealthy or for that matter healthy,*
> *If your heart's alright, you'll do!*

> J. G.

∙∙∙

To ponder:
How 'much of a Christian' am I? Would my verdict on myself be
upheld by those who know me?

Time for Tears?

'When Jesus saw her weeping, and the Jews who had come along with her also weeping, he was deeply moved in spirit and troubled . . . Jesus wept' (vv. 33, 35).

Believers sometimes feel their faith means they should not shed tears on sad occasions. At the time of Jesus, however, outward expression of grief was the order of the day. Loud wailing was expected. Everyone seems to know that the shortest verse in the Bible is 'Jesus wept', but did Jesus weep because he had arrived after Lazarus had died, or were his tears for Mary and Martha, who had lost a brother? Or was he simply grieving his own loss of a good friend? Whatever the reason, it is clearly permissible to cry.

There is a Time for Tears

The sun won't always shine,
Sometimes rain clouds form;
After the clearest sky
May come the thunderstorm.
Unexpected stress
Awakens sleeping fears
And faith must find its way
Through mists of bitter tears.
There is a time for tears, a time for sighing.
There is a place for grief, a place for crying.
But in the mystery of unanswered prayers,
Let faith hold fast to this: God cares!

Pleasing God?

* *

' "I praise you, Father, Lord of heaven and earth, because you have hidden these things from the wise and learned, and revealed them to little children. Yes, Father, for this was your good pleasure" ' (v. 21).

Genesis 1:26 tells us God said: ' "Let us make man in our image, in our likeness." ' Clearly the intention was to make human beings as much like God as is humanly possible. The hope must have been that we would somehow reflect something of the glory of God.

Surely it was not God's intention that he should become like us in our ugliness, so why do we all too often bring him down to our level? Perhaps it is to help us disguise, or even justify, our failings.

The Old Testament talks about God being a vengeful God who likes to get his own back: I have a problem with this. Revenge and jealousy are ugly human characteristics and I do not see them reflected in the face of Christ, who told us that when we see him we see the Father. To present a picture of our all-wise and all-loving Father losing his temper suggests he does little better than me when it comes to self-control. I don't believe that.

Other very human but more credible reactions are seen in the Father who the Son has so beautifully revealed. In Jesus we see qualities we are relieved to discover. There is tenderness, compassion, sympathy. We instinctively sense that when we are close to Jesus we are near to God.

When we see these same qualities in human beings are we also seeing God there, in those ordinary faces? When we watch someone weep over another's misery, is it the compassion of God we are witnessing? Does God himself rejoice that his nature is thus reflected?

In our study passage today we see ordinary children of God working miracles – for their Father's 'good pleasure' (v. 21). Have I pleased my Father in a similar way lately? Have you?

* *

I believe that God the Father can be seen in God the Son,
In the gentleness of Jesus love for all the world is shown.

J. G.

International Charity

'"Love the Lord your God with all your heart and with all
your soul and with all your strength and with all your mind";
and, "Love your neighbour as yourself"' (v. 27).

This story told by Jesus is probably the best-known piece of teaching in the world. Even people who know almost nothing else about the Bible have heard of the 'good Samaritan' for this two-word phrase has become part of the English vocabulary. To call someone a 'good Samaritan' is high praise.

The Teacher taught us so much through this short story. Through it Jesus applauds the expression of love for God, who is thought to be beyond us, and for our neighbour, who is beside us.

Need is an all-embracing, world-encompassing thing. The victims of robbers and the generous Samaritans who help them sometimes have little in common except their humanity. But in times of stress there can be no discrimination. Charity has no place for jingoism.

In recent years deaths through terrorism in New York and tsunamis in south Asia were both met with a flood of compassion and selfless generosity from all corners of the world. Clearly, humankind is not incapable of charity – which is, after all, another word for love.

But charity is more than a moment's kindliness. That of the Samaritan included the use of his own transport, the gift of his own healing ointment and hotel accommodation for as long as it was needed. All for a foreigner!

The Samaritan said to the innkeeper, '"Look after him . . . and when I return, I will reimburse you for any extra expense you may have"' (v. 35). Was this the kind of 'second mile' that Jesus mentioned (Matthew 5:41, 42)? Jesus always personified his teaching.

Love suffereth patiently;
Love worketh silently;
Love seeketh not her own.
Love never faileth;
Love still prevaileth,
Lord, in me thy love enthrone!
Arch R. Wiggins

High Commendation

* *

'"But a Samaritan, as he travelled, came where the man was; and when he saw him, he took pity on him. He went to him and bandaged his wounds, pouring on oil and wine"' (vv. 33, 34).

The story of the good Samaritan came as a huge surprise to those who first heard it. After the shortcomings of the priest and the Levite were rebuked, a third traveller was introduced. As a Samaritan he would have been despised by the Jewish listeners, and when it became clear that the Teacher was making the Samaritan the hero of his story there must have been loud opposition, or at the very least a frosty silence. But Jesus insisted on choosing a 'foreigner' to play the role of the impeccable neighbour, and commended him for it.

What did the Samaritan do? He crossed the road to assess the victim's need. Not a pretty sight! He bandaged him, but first poured into the wounds both healing oil and wine. Not cheap! He gave the man the only donkey available, then took him to an inn, giving two silver coins – two days' wages – to the innkeeper to pay for his continuing care. And he went even further, promising to pay any expenses in excess of that when he passed that way again.

Was it with an innocent look on his face that Jesus asked his listeners who was the hero of the story? Neighbourliness is not measured by nationality, race or religion. It is the compassionate person who goes the second mile at personal cost who hears the applause of Christ. Christians who desire to win the smile of their Lord should remember his words, referring to the Samaritan: '"Go and do likewise"' (v. 37).

To ponder:
What 'sort' of person would we spend two days' wages on? Family? Of course! A good friend? Sometimes. A stranger? An outcast? Where is the limit of our generosity? What bounds does it know?

Chosen Well

....

'"Only one thing is needed. Mary has chosen what is better,
and it will not be taken away from her"' (v. 42).

The thoughts of Christ are often revealed in his parables. Sometimes his feelings are understood when the observer notes his reaction to a particular situation or person. Here Jesus speaks his mind directly and there is no possibility of misunderstanding. Mary's choice has the approval of Jesus and no one will be allowed to take it from her.

Jesus was not trying to demolish Martha or bring her to tears, but he wanted to make it clear that spiritual needs are more important than physical requirements, and we must make time to meet them whenever we can.

Jesus might have used the same words he spoke to his followers when they were over-anxious about food and left their tired and hungry Teacher to bare his heart to an 'undesirable' spiritual seeker alone. On their return they thought their leader looked refreshed. Could someone have brought him food? Jesus told them: '"I have food to eat that you know nothing about"' (John 4:32, 33). It seems Martha knew nothing about it either, but Mary did!

Two significant phrases are found in Luke 10:39, 40 which underline the differences between these two women. Mary sat at the feet of her Teacher, *listening*. Here was an incomparable opportunity for her to be taught new truth, discover the things that matter most and learn what discipleship demands. Martha chose otherwise and received a rebuke, albeit a loving one.

Mary concentrated on her Lord. Martha focused on the menu and her reputation for hospitality. In so doing, Martha was *distracted* from a chance of a lifetime. Jesus' rebuke recognised her good intentions: '"You are worried and upset about many things, but only one thing is needed"' (vv. 41, 42).

This homely picture is vividly drawn and calls us to give attention to our priorities. Spiritual communication with Christ is not an option but an essential for every Christian. We just have to refuse to be distracted!

Persistent Prayer

'"So I say to you: Ask and it will be given to you; seek and you will find; knock and the door will be opened to you"' (v. 9).

Observation over a long period has taught me that children quickly learn to know they have only to ask to receive. Their limited vocabulary does not prevent them from making their wants known. What they lack in words they make up in volume. The bawling child in the supermarket knows instinctively the importance of persistence and acts accordingly. Most children quickly master the method of embarrassing the parent and add this tool effectively to their armoury.

I'm not for a moment suggesting we should try this ruse upon the Almighty! There is no need, and it would not work. The Christ is not offended by the persistence of his people. He applauds it. It proves the seriousness of our request and reveals our confidence in the divine Creator to provide for our needs. Our continuing requests are understood as a compliment. Jesus says as much in his parable of the widow who wearied an unjust judge with her requests until she got what she wanted (Luke 18:1–8).

God is neither unjust nor unwilling. The regular request does not need to reach the height of irritation for it to be noticed. We can't embarrass our God into action. The angels in heaven probably chuckle at our attempts to do so!

Persistence in prayer is a good exercise for us all. It is a valuable way for us to focus on our most important needs and discard the frivolous ones. Too often we bother God with minor issues we could easily solve for ourselves with a little effort.

I remember an excellent Christian comic who in one humorous routine called a prayer meeting to decide which cabbage it was God's will for us to buy. I know time is infinite in heaven but it is short-lived on earth. We shouldn't waste it, should we?

Behold the throne of grace, the promise calls me near;
There Jesus shows a smiling face and waits to answer prayer.
John Newton

Count the Cost in Advance

'"If he lays the foundation and is not able to finish it, everyone who sees it will ridicule him, saying, 'This fellow began to build and was not able to finish'"' (vv. 29, 30).

Our Lord firmly believed that all his would-be disciples should count in advance the likely costs of such a venture. Jesus hid nothing in this respect. He was totally honest. No cheap discipleship was ever offered. Cross-bearing and close following of Christ were the first requirements.

When some of his followers discovered the high price of the privilege that was theirs, they resigned. Somebody less than Jesus would have tried to coax them back to the ranks. But Jesus asked the others if they wished to go home too! Realism was essential from the start in the Church of Christ.

There's more. Christ continues: '"Any of you who does not give up everything he has cannot be my disciple"' (v. 33). No wonder there are few queues outside churches.

I hear it said in some parts of the world that congregations are small because the churches don't use the most modern music, don't organise enough entertainment, don't have comfortable buildings or don't illustrate their sermons with clever audio-visual aids. But these are not the real reasons why so many congregations are small. They are small because people have discovered that Christianity is a demanding thing.

Who wants to give up everything, carry a cross and humbly serve sometimes unpleasant people? Particularly when it emerges that such sacrifice is a seven-day-a-week thing – not an activity occupying one hour on Sundays spent sitting in a pew.

People often ask me why The Salvation Army exists. That's easy. It all began with a statement made by a seventeen-year-old Nottingham lad: 'God shall have all there is of William Booth.' William counted the cost in advance and never went back on his willingness to accept it. Jesus approved, and The Salvation Army was the result.

To ponder:
Are we prepared for expensive discipleship?

Love Me, Simon?

*'When they had finished eating, Jesus said to Simon Peter,
"Simon son of John, do you truly love me . . . ?"' (v. 15).*

This brief conversation between Jesus and Simon Peter is so private
that perhaps we should not eavesdrop. The Christ knew Simon
loved him. These moments were designed to assure Simon that Jesus
loved *him*.

Jesus:
Simon Peter, talk to me,
Tell me what your eyes can see.
Can you glimpse a future? You?
Don't deceive me if you do.
Do you love me? Yes or no?
Tell me, and I'll let you go.

Peter:
Yes! I love you but I've failed;
Watched you thorny-crowned and nailed,
Saw them laughing in your face;
And you saw my damned disgrace.
How could I be silent? How?
I have nothing to say now!

Jesus:
Love declares, and love decides,
And love never fakes or hides.
Just one question I request;
Answer, tell me, be your best:
I know that you love me still,
Would you love to do my will?

Peter:
Look, my tears are flowing now;
No more lies, I don't know how.
More than others, more than all,
I love you. I'm at your call.
I can't put it into verse.
Yours for better, yours for worse.

Jesus:
Never doubt my love for you.
Pentecost is coming through,
You've got sacred work to do!

Undesirable Duties?

'"You also, when you have done everything you were told to do, should say, 'We are unworthy servants; we have only done our duty'"' (v. 10).

Too often we fall into the mistake of supposing the disciples of today are not of the same calibre as yesterday's people, but those early-day followers of Christ were not perfect either. Peter, following the arrest of his Lord, to save his own skin swore he did not know Jesus. And 'Doubting' Thomas, after missing out on one of Jesus' resurrection appearances, wanted proof that would leave him without any need for faith at all. But once they recognised their responsibilities, nothing could stop them. Thereafter they always 'did their duty', even to death.

Like hundreds of thousands of British citizens of my generation I spent two years on military service. It led me to learn a new vocabulary, which included 'skivers'. A skiver was someone who went to great lengths to avoid doing his or her duty.

In Christian circles you can always recognise skivers. They're always wanting to rewrite their contract with Jesus. The fact is, that contract is pretty clear. Here's my version of it, based on Matthew 16:24–28: 'Anybody who wants to be in my lot must leave self behind, pick up their cross and come with me wherever I take them.'

Those who accept that contract never mention things like reward and never go on strike. It's easy to recognise the truly dutiful. Easy-going people, they cheerfully go the extra mile.

J. B. Phillips's translation of Luke 17:10 puts it beautifully: '"When you have done everything that you are told to do, you can say, 'We are not much good as servants; we have only done what we ought to do.'"'

William Booth, founder of The Salvation Army, was fond of telling his troops: 'That and better will do.' It might have seemed like grudging praise, but he was right!

To ponder:
Do we deliver everything we promise to God? Good intentions are not enough.

Courtesy Commended

....

'"Were not all ten cleansed? Where are the other nine? Was no-one found to return and give praise to God except this foreigner?"' (v. 17).

It was a Thursday in Camberwell, London, and the platform of the Salvation Army hall was crowded with more than 200 officer-cadets in training to become Salvation Army ministers. I was among them. As usual, Commissioner Frederick Coutts, principal of the training college, faced a packed congregation. To everyone's surprise he called a shy young woman to the rostrum to speak to us all. She was trembling at the opportunity before her and made small mistakes in vocabulary or grammar, one after another.

A ripple of laughter came from the student body. The principal sat on the edge of his chair and leaned forward as if he was listening to something profound. A second wave of laughter was silenced as his sad and angry eyes swept over the platform. He turned back to give the girl his full attention and when she concluded he stood up to thank her for what she had shared with us. Like a conjurer, he drew out what was probably the only beautiful and profound thing she had said and with genuine gratitude held it up to the light.

The girl smiled. We students were not too comfortable. We had learned that courtesy and kindliness are marks of the true Christian. Politeness is the privilege of all God's people.

When Jesus healed ten lepers of their fearful disease all were cured but only one returned to express his gratitude. 'He threw himself at Jesus' feet and thanked him' (v. 16). The Healer could not help but point out that the courteous man was a despised Samaritan. The outcast was the gentleman of the day. As the proverb reminds us: 'Handsome is as handsome does.'

To say thank you to the giver is not an optional thing, however small the gift. Silence in such circumstances is shameful. When King Lear's two older daughters withheld their gratitude he declared: 'Blow! Blow thou winter's wind. Thou art not so unkind as man's ingratitude.'

Our occasional silence to God for his goodness shames us.

Penitent People

....

'The tax collector stood at a distance. He would not even
look up to heaven, but beat his breast and said, "God, have
mercy on me, a sinner"' (v. 13).

When George Bernard Shaw wrote about former burglars giving their testimonies at Salvation Army meetings he insisted they should be 'as burglarious as possible'. Certainly his play *Major Barbara* is nothing if not black and white. All the characters are clearly either good or bad.

Jesus takes a similar approach in this story. It helps to make the message plain. The Pharisee is as Pharisaical as could be and the tax collector clearly a crook. The Pharisee could not be more inappropriately proud and pious. If it was a pantomime the audience would boo him, while the tax collector would be cheered for his sincere penitence.

Christ approved of penitence and his Church does too. The Anglicans teach me that the truly penitent is absolved. The Roman Catholics tell me a confessional is helpful. The Salvation Army's 'altar' is called the mercy seat or penitent's form. There anyone is free to kneel and pray for pardon, purity and power – though such prayers can be offered equally validly anywhere at all. Promises are often made there. Private communication with a ready-to-listen God awaits any seeker there.

In Jesus' story the tax collector did everything right. He was hesitant to ask for pardon, and in humility stayed at a distance from the altar. He would not look God in the face but beat his breast to express his shame and regret. He admitted his failures. He asked for mercy and he got it. That experience can be ours too. As Jesus said: '"He who humbles himself will be exalted"' (v. 14).

....

> Thou art coming to a King,
> Large petitions with thee bring.
> For his grace and power are such
> None can ever ask too much.
> *John Newton*

Sacred Investment

··

'"He was made king, however, and returned home. Then he sent for the servants to whom he had given the money, in order to find out what they had gained with it. The first one came and said, 'Sir, your mina has earned ten more'"' (vv. 15, 16).

It's interesting to note the different accounts of this parable of Jesus. The writers of the Gospels of Luke and Matthew seem to remember different details (compare Luke 19 with Matthew 25:14–30). Luke recalls identical amounts being given to the servants, Matthew's memory is of varying amounts being distributed. Luke refers to a king but Matthew mentions no king.

Such variations in memory are very human, and the basic principles of the story are the same. The servants in both accounts are expected to use and enlarge their capacities. Luke makes the instructions to them very clear: 'Put this money to work until I come back' (v. 13). They knew what they had to do.

The commendation of the successful investors and the criticism of the poor performers are the same in both accounts. Success was rewarded with increased responsibility. The end of the indolent servants was sad indeed (and surely not to be taken literally!).

Jesus' message is clear: we have all received precious assets. Youth has its riches, but experience is equally valuable. We have faithful friends, opportunities to study, chances to serve those with greater needs than ourselves, time to reflect. We have time for prayer, and some have wisdom to counsel others, a gift for making music or other artistic capacities – perhaps the ability to write well or to make a garden beautiful.

These gifts are meant to be developed to the full. Not to invest them is a shame, if not a sin, for it deprives other people of joy. Good investors are among the happiest people. Our Lord approves of that!

··

To ponder:
Are our God-given talents hard at work, mothballed or wrapped-up in cotton wool and only rarely utilised? On judgment day we will not be able to plead ignorance of God's expectations.

Duty Done?

....

*'He saw through their duplicity and said to them, "Show me
a denarius. Whose portrait and inscription are on it?" "Caesar's,"
they replied. He said to them, "Then give to Caesar what is Caesar's,
and to God what is God's" ' (vv. 23–25).*

I was not the most proficient Scout, but I've never forgotten the
promises I made to 'do my duty to God and the king'. I took 'the king'
to mean my country and I had no problems with that. A few years later
my sovereign drew attention to my duty to give two years of my life to
National Service and I did as I was required, not unhappily.

Duty is not a popular word in the world of today. Not all parents
accept responsibility for their offspring and some children avoid their
duty to ageing parents. Some citizens try to avoid paying taxes, or the
fare on buses and trains. If successful they feel they have done
something clever, but each of us has a responsibility to contribute to
the society in which we live, particularly in respect of supporting those
in need.

Christians should be models where the fulfilment of duty is
concerned, even if it brings ridicule for our honesty. Jesus had
something to say about it when questioned by people seeking to trip
him up. His answer is still a good one: 'Give to Caesar what is Caesar's,
and to God what is God's.'

....

> There's a path that's sometimes thorny,
> There's a narrow way, and straight;
> It is called the path of duty,
> And it leads to Heaven's gate.
> While we tread this path of duty,
> We will find our needs supplied
> From the river of God's mercy
> That is flowing close beside.
>   *Sidney Edward Cox*

Out of Poverty

* * *

'"All these people gave their gifts out of their wealth; but she out of her poverty put in all she had to live on"' (v. 4).

Generosity, says Jesus, is to be measured according to how much the giver could have given and how much is left in store. It was with this measure in mind that Jesus said: 'I tell you the truth, this poor widow has put in more than all the others' (v. 3). Sometimes when a large present is offered it is not really worthy to be called a 'gift' – it is simply a public relations gesture.

At the time of Jesus the massive trumpet-shaped collection boxes at the Temple in Jerusalem were designed to make an attractive ringing sound when large coins were tossed in from a distance. Did the poor widow quietly slip her contribution in so as not to be noticed? Many churches provide envelopes for regular offerings during services. Do they spare us from the temptation to flourish our generosity . . . or allow us to disguise our inappropriately modest contributions? Forgive my intrusive questions. I would never have mentioned the subject had Jesus not brought it up!

Charitable gifts which have a sacrificial element about them are double-blessed. The 'hurting' aspect of the widow's two copper coins touches our hearts and perhaps influences how deep we delve in our pockets. We note Jesus' commendation of her.

But it is not only with money that we must learn to be generous. People are sometimes in desperate need of our time and attention. To give advice or simply lend someone your ear are precious gifts. Sympathy is particularly precious. We should give it generously.

* * *

All to Jesus I surrender,
All to him I freely give;
I will ever love and trust him,
In his presence daily live.
I surrender all, I surrender all,
All to thee, my blessed Saviour,
I surrender all.

Judson Ven de Venter

I Believe in Hope

'These three remain: faith, hope and love. But the greatest of these is love' (v. 13).

I won't argue with anyone over this: the greatest *is* love. But hope is a great thing too – an essential thing. Love that is hopeless is not all it could be.

Love Comes with Hope

When I'm alone, when I feel weakest,
When in my own strength I know I'll fail;
When things around are at their bleakest
And those I trusted I find are frail –
He comes with hope, my living Saviour.
My cry for help is not ignored.
Acknowledged need is met with mercy;
Our close communion is restored.
When Jesus comes, my night is ended.
To all my darkness he is my dawn.
He knows me well, he's understanding;
My faith's re-founded; my hope reborn.

Beware!

Introduction

When Jesus warns us of the dangers which surround us he does so not merely to scold, and certainly not to threaten. Always he speaks with compassion. His purpose is to reveal to us the traps which could bring us harm, and to show us how they can be avoided. Jesus was subject to powerful temptation himself and calls us to be aware of the strength of the forces which oppose our efforts to be the people God would have us be.

Jesus' warnings sometimes take us by surprise. Even our friends can lead us in the wrong direction. Vigilance is needed always. But we don't call Jesus 'Saviour' for nothing. We should not be reluctant to call for his help. If anyone knows what it is like to be human, he does!

> I'm only human;
> Please remember that.
> I have my limitations
> After all.
> It's not surprising,
> Not to me at least,
> That now and then I falter
> Or I fall.
>
> I'm only human,
> But you're the expert
> Who chose to call himself
> The Son of Man,
> And made a study of
> Our frail condition.
> If anyone can understand,
> You can!

Self-sufficient?

....

Jesus answered, "It is written: 'Man does not live on bread alone, but on every word that comes from the mouth of God'"' (v. 4).

It's generally agreed by Bible translators that the Greek word usually rendered as 'tempted' might just as correctly be translated as 'tested'. Satan, the accuser, is God's enemy, dedicated to the defeat of God's people. In the course of this he subjects us regularly to strict testing. For Satan to be defeated we need more than our own human strength – something more than 'bread' (v. 3). Those under attack need divine, spiritual reinforcements – every bit of support that comes from God (v. 4).

The warning from Jesus here is to beware of self-sufficiency, bearing in mind that forces of evil invariably focus on our weaknesses. We need God's guidance, direction, empowering. God's testing of us aims to make us aware of both our strengths and weaknesses, and encourages us to prepare accordingly. Satan's testing underlines our weakness and tends to shatter our confidence.

These verses reveal that God incarnate was not exempt from such attack, and we do well to observe his strategy for protection and imitate it.

It is part of the cunning of evil to reach us even through our friends. Christ himself experienced this when his friend Peter tried to dissuade him from the very idea of crucifixion: 'Jesus turned and said to Peter, "Get behind me, Satan!"' (Matthew 16:23). Satan adopts innumerable disguises, sometimes employing the most innocent of people as his agents.

Another strategy of evil is to leave us alone now and then so that we drop our guard, thinking we are safe. Luke's Gospel says: 'When the devil had finished all this tempting, he left him until an opportune time' (4:13). Many of us could tell of defeat due to the 'opportune' time that temptation struck. The King James translation tells us the devil 'departed from him for a season'. Would that be the hunting season? The holiday season? Don't be deceived; any time is testing time for the prince of darkness. Beware! Summon reinforcements.

Good for Nothing?

....

' *"You are the salt of the earth. But if the salt loses its saltiness, how can it be made salty again? It is no longer good for anything"' (v. 13).*

In New Testament times salt was precious and prized. Things could be bought with salt. When Jesus talked of salt he was, in a way, referring to a kind of wealth. Also, salt liberated flavour and was an essential means of preserving meat and fish. So it was immensely useful as well as precious.

For those listening to Jesus, most of their salt came from the Dead Sea. This was not the purest source so the salt was not always of the highest quality and when it lost its saltiness it was a general catastrophe as well as a domestic disaster.

In likening his people to salt Jesus was offering a compliment. They were to be purifying and health-giving elements in the world. But when salt lost its essential saltiness its raison d'être had gone. As Jesus said, ' "It is no longer good for anything, except to be thrown out and trampled by men"' (v. 13).

When a Christian exhibits such seeping away of Christly beauty it must be a huge disappointment for that individual's friends. But it is a truly mega-disappointment for Christ, who hopes for great things from us. The people named Christians are called to demonstrate sincerity, integrity, compassion, sympathy, tolerance, generosity, mercy, purity. In short, Christlikeness. If we fail to do this, what value have we any more?

Christ warns us not to allow these qualities to evaporate. The danger is that their gradual disappearance is not noticed by the person most concerned. But good friends might observe it. Would it be a kindness for a sensitive friend to draw his or her attention to the growing loss before it is too late?

Is there a point of no return or can the prodigal always return home and regain what he or she has lost? Jesus gives us a gloriously positive answer: ' "With man this is impossible, but with God all things are possible"' (Matthew 19:26). Where there's life there's hope!

Not a Word!

....

' "When you give to the needy, do not let your left hand know what your right hand is doing, so that your giving may be in secret" ' (v. 3).

Anyone involved in fundraising knows the power of publicity. Some donors will give more if their generosity is publicly acknowledged. They want their gift not just to help the cause but to generate applause. Christ is not impressed by such giving. He says of such people: ' "I tell you the truth, they have received their reward in full" ' (v. 2). In other words they've got what they wanted, and that's all they're going to get!

Although generous donations – given for whatever reason – can encourage others to be similarly generous, the donors who earn the Master's approval are those who make it a condition that their generosity receives no publicity. Even their left hand, says Jesus, must not be told what the right hand has done – a memorable phrase, like so many Jesus coined.

Giving should be done, said Jesus, in the same way that praying should be done – in secret. And the same is true of fasting. In Jesus' day some who fasted drew attention to their piety by dressing in sackcloth-and-ashes fashion. Jesus did not approve: ' "When you fast, put oil on your head and wash your face, so that it will not be obvious to men that you are fasting, but only to your Father, who is unseen" ' (v. 17).

God will notice. We need no one else's approval.

....

No longer in bondage, my freedom I'll use
My Master to serve in the way he shall choose;
To work or to witness, to go or remain,
His smile of approval my infinite gain.
Earth's pleasures and treasures no longer allure,
My spirit aspires to the things which endure;
To walk with my Saviour in garments of white,
My highest ambition, my constant delight.
                                        Charles Coller

Dangerous Diversions

••

' "No-one can serve two masters. Either he will hate the one and love the other, or he will be devoted to the one and despise the other. You cannot serve both God and Money" ' (v. 24).

I recognise three important choices in the teaching of Jesus. The first is the choice between what is temporary and what is permanent. Material things, by their nature, are not lasting. They decay. Moth and rust destroy them. They can be stolen. A house can burn down. Christ tells us to choose the things which survive eternally – spiritual things. They may be invisible but they are the most precious, and we should treasure them, for, says Jesus: ' "Where your treasure is, there your heart will be also" ' (v. 21).

The second thing to choose is light over darkness. Our spiritual eyes are beyond price: ' "If your eyes are good, your whole body will be full of light" ' (v. 22). That light dispels the darkness of ignorance, which will otherwise prevent us from experiencing anything of value. Jesus said: ' "I am the light of the world. Whoever follows me will never walk in darkness, but will have the light of life" ' (John 8:12). It's our choice. Why walk in the dark?

The third decision is who or what will rule our life. We can have only one master. To attempt to serve two is a recipe for chaos and disaster. As the proverb puts it: 'He who chases two rabbits catches none.' How up-to-date and relevant Jesus is when he identifies the pursuit of wealth as a danger zone: 'You cannot serve both God and Money.'

••

To ponder:
Joshua challenged the Israelites with words that have echoed down the centuries ever since: 'Choose for yourselves this day whom you will serve' (Joshua 24:15). In fact, 'this day' is every day. Every day, situations arise which require us to reconfirm our commitment to Christ by choosing the right and refusing the wrong. May God help us!

Your Father Knows

• •

'"Do not worry about tomorrow, for tomorrow will worry about itself.
Each day has enough trouble of its own"' (v. 34).

Most of us worry too much, unnecessarily. When I was a boy, living in a small English country town, the Salvation Army congregation I belonged to included a number of part-time members of the fire brigade. Every now and then, often halfway through the sermon, the fire station siren sounded and the firemen immediately dashed for the door of the hall, as it was their duty to respond as quickly as possible.

They were always followed out of the door by a woman member of the congregation, wearing a very worried face. Was she, too, a vital member of the fire service? No, she always left to check it wasn't her home that was on fire! I'm afraid we boys giggled. We should have had sympathy for her.

A much-respected friend of mine, whenever he leaves his home, worries that he has failed to lock the door properly and invariably returns to check. I carefully make no comment when, breathlessly, he catches me up.

Are we regularly attacked by minor worries? Would today be a good day to dismiss them? When Jesus says, 'Love your neighbour' we take his words seriously. Should we not listen equally attentively to what he says about our attitude to worry? Jesus asks us, '"Who of you by worrying can add a single hour to his life."' (v. 27)? Who indeed? Little things we can't change should not be allowed to worry us.

Jesus tells us our Father-God, who cares deeply about us, knows about our concerns (v. 32). We should not let the possibility of sorrow tomorrow damage our serenity today.

Someone has said that worry is the premium we pay for things which may never happen. Jesus would agree – but urges us to ensure our priorities are in order, making sure we are seeking first his kingdom. Then we can simply trust him to meet our needs, both in this life and eternally.

The Plank in My Eye

' "Why do you look at the speck of sawdust in your brother's eye and pay no attention to the plank in your own eye? How can you say to your brother, 'Let me take the speck out of your eye,' when all the time there is a plank in your own eye? You hypocrite" ' (vv. 3–5).

We know Jesus was in favour of those who hesitated to pronounce judgment against others. He approved of those who withheld condemnation. He commended people who were quick to forgive. He had little time for hypocrites who offered to correct other people's errors while making no efforts to put right their own failings.

The best of us have to admit that sometimes we judge too quickly and without grounds. Too many Sunday congregations include a forest of planks protruding from the eyes of worshippers who have had a judge-and-jury week. A few moments of penitence should be offered to get rid of the timber!

Leslie Weatherhead tells of a headmaster in the north of England who, without asking if there were an explanation, caned every boy who was late. Having beaten one little fellow who had never been late before, the headmaster learnt that the boy had been to a coal mine to get news of his brother after a colliery explosion. The brother was brought up to the pit-head dead and, having identified him, the younger lad went to school and was late. What an awful verdict and punishment must have resulted from the master's judgment on himself!

We have all been too quick, on occasion, to come to a wrong conclusion. Sometimes we have been able to seek pardon from the victim of our hasty judgment. Sometimes that opportunity has been denied us. Our haste to criticise says a great deal about ourselves.

We're all seeking the same Saviour,
We're all seeking the self-same Lord.
We're all claiming the same cleansing,
We're all finding our peace restored.

J. G.

Divine Antidote

* *

' "I have told you all this so that you might find your peace in me.
You will find trouble in the world – but, never lose heart,
I have conquered the world!" ' (v. 31, JBP).

When Jesus warns us that we shall have trouble, it is not to distress us but to prepare us to face it. By prayer we shall find our peace in him, and through him we shall not be crushed. Our Lord says, ' "Ask now, and you will receive, that your joy may be overflowing" ' (v. 24, *JBP*).

A Very Human Thing

I don't want you to nurse me,
But I'm glad
You come along beside me
When I'm sad.
Depression is a very
Human thing.
I should know better and not
Let it sting.
You often warn me when it's
On its way
And you invite me, Lord, to
Come and pray.
Point out the traps that await me –
Please, Lord, do!
I'd come to grief if it were
Not for you.
My worst temptations simply
Have to scram!
No plaster saint but I'm a
Better man!

Filled with Awe

....

'Knowing their thoughts, Jesus said, "Why do you entertain evil thoughts in your hearts? Which is easier: to say, 'Your sins are forgiven,' or to say, 'Get up and walk'?"' (vv. 4, 5).

Healers come in many forms: family doctor, surgeon, psychiatrist, herbalist, acupuncturist, physiotherapist, faith healer. Some heal by medication, some by touch, some by counselling, some by prayer. The Gospels tell us that Jesus also used more than one method of healing. Sometimes he touched the person, sometimes he spoke to them. Sometimes he healed them from a distance without them even being aware of his actions. Only he knows why he varied his methods.

This story of the paralysed man is an interesting one. First we have the faith of the man himself, who agreed – or perhaps asked – to be manhandled along the busy, roughly surfaced street to where Jesus was. Then we have the faith of his friends who carried him to Jesus on his mat. Finally we have the teachers of the law who looked on. These outwardly ultra-religious men should have had the greatest faith of all, but Jesus rebuked them because they entertained 'evil thoughts' in their hearts (v. 4).

How did Jesus react? 'Take heart, son,' he told the paralysed man, 'your sins are forgiven' (v. 2). The Lord recognised the nature of the man's problem. It is as true today as then that people can become physically ill through the stress of guilt and remorse over past mistakes, which they may or may not see as sin. Only forgiveness brings relief and healing. Psychiatrists know that today. Jesus knew it 2,000 years ago.

'Your sins are forgiven' was all the man needed to hear. But for the sake of those who listened and scoffed, Jesus made the consequences of that forgiveness plain: 'Get up, take your mat and go home,' he told the man. The Gospel writer records he did just that. Looking on, 'the crowd . . . were filled with awe' (v. 8) and gave God the glory.

From time to time down the years I've seen people made well after asking for and receiving forgiveness through Jesus. Sometimes the change has been marginal, sometimes dramatic. When it happens, everyone should take care where the glory goes.

Penitence Withheld

'Jesus began to denounce the cities in which most of his miracles had been performed, because they did not repent' (v. 20).

This passage suggests that our failure to repent when given the opportunity to do so is eternally dangerous. Our Saviour-God delights to pardon when sincere regret and the desire to reform are evident but, sadly, some people express regret for their weakness or wickedness but display no evidence of changed behaviour.

These verses tell us that the people of the cities mentioned were condemned because they rejected the opportunity for absolution. They all had the opportunity to experience the liberty and joy which comes from pardon received. They had seen God incarnate; they had heard his message; they had watched as people's lives were transformed through the physical and spiritual healing of sick people. But they chose not to change their behaviour.

Pardon is more than weeping. I have seen tears fall from seemingly repentant people who subsequently displayed no evidence, through changed behaviour, of having received God's gracious forgiveness.

Says Jesus: ' "If the miracles that were performed in you had been performed in Sodom, it would have remained to this day" ' (v. 23). The implication is that we should take the opportunity when it comes our way to repent and reform, lest we face the punishment that befell that sinful city.

There are times for cities to repent of the awful things that happen within their walls, and times, too, when whole congregations should be penitent. But usually the need is for individuals to forgive each other. Repentance is most precious when a person regrets his or her failure to be what God wants them to be. The warning words of Christ were spoken not to hurt us but to heal us.

A prayer:
'Forgive all my blindness and folly, my prodigal wanderings and shame. O heed now the outcrying pains of my heart! I come as the prodigal came.'

Evangeline Booth

Priceless Metaphors

....

'"The kingdom of heaven is like treasure hidden in a field . . . like a merchant looking for fine pearls"' (vv. 44, 45).

I'm glad the Master went to some pains to explain the kingdom of heaven. His metaphors shed light on one of Christianity's most precious mysteries. Jesus loved to paint pictures for our minds to dwell on, but such a massive subject as the kingdom of heaven needs more than one picture to convey its many facets.

The kingdom is like a hidden treasure and a priceless pearl. It's like the tiny mustard seed from which great trees can grow. It is the yeast which generates growth in that which looks lifeless. It is a fishing net, a field of wheat which weeds want to invade. It's like all these things and more.

The kingdom is what God is and where God reigns. It is a thing of staggering beauty and brilliant light and endless joy and infinite knowledge. It is a priceless thing, so valuable that if we had any sense we would sell everything we own to have it and to be in it.

The metaphors of hidden treasure and a priceless pearl are similar yet different. In the first we see a man finding by chance something of value in a field that doesn't belong to him. In the second someone finds what he (or she) has long been searching for. Here's the similarity: both sold all they had to own – and be owned by – what they had found. They came from different directions to the same destination. Jesus said that would happen: '"They shall come from the east, and from the west, and from the north, and from the south, and shall sit down in the kingdom of God!"' (Luke 13:29, *KJV*).

....

To ponder (or sing!):

> I've found the pearl of greatest price,
> My heart doth sing for joy;
> And sing I must, for Christ I have,
> O what a Christ have I!

> *John Mason*

A Varied Menu

'"The kingdom of heaven is like a net that was let down into the lake and caught all kinds of fish. When it was full, the fishermen pulled it up on the shore. Then they sat down and collected the good fish in baskets, but threw the bad away"' (vv. 47, 48).

Every fisherman knows more than one way of catching fish. Different bait is selected according to the kind of fish he hopes to catch, and while for sea or lake fishing a net is often best, for the angler standing on a riverbank or waist-deep in fast-running water, a rod and fly can be the answer. It's an exciting moment when we feel the line tugging as a fish bites. The expert fisherman knows the best conditions for success, but skill and patience are always needed.

Once, when his disciples were disappointed after trying and failing to catch fish, Jesus gave advice which enabled them to bring in a huge catch (Luke 5:4–10). Later, after he told them their mission would be to 'catch' men and women, they must have thought back to that occasion and that advice. Skill and patience are just as vital when evangelising.

Those of us who take seriously Christ's great commission to take his message to all the world do well to follow his advice and teaching, remembering that all kinds of people can become fishers of all kinds of people in all kinds of ways. Whatever works is the way to do it – even if the 'bait' or method is a new departure that doesn't immediately appeal to us.

As Jesus, changing the metaphor, goes on to tell his disciples: '"Every teacher of the law who has been instructed about the kingdom of heaven is like the owner of a house who brings out of his storeroom new treasures as well as old"' (v. 52). Those who dislike change can't opt out, but perhaps they can take heart from the words 'as well as'!

To ponder:
What metaphor of the kingdom of heaven most appeals to you? But remember, no metaphor will be as great as the real thing!

The Truly Clean

....

> ' "Listen and understand. What goes into a man's mouth does
> not make him 'unclean', but what comes out of his mouth,
> that is what makes him 'unclean' " ' (v. 10).

When Jesus spoke these words to a crowd, his disciples told him: ' "Do you know that the Pharisees were offended when they heard this?" ' (v. 12). I don't think Jesus needed to be told. He knew all about the importance given to cleanliness in the ceremonies and rules of the religion of his time.

To walk over a grave made the walker unclean. If someone failed to wash his hands before eating, the food was ritually polluted. The accidental eating of certain kinds of meat made the eater contaminated. The Pharisees covered their drinking water in case something dirty found its way in and disqualified the drinker from approaching God.

Jesus told the crowd that believing this is to get it all wrong. It's the 'inside' of a person which is clean or unclean. It's within the spirit of a person that uncleanness develops, to emerge, damage and contaminate others. Cruel criticism, dishonest words, attitudes, thoughts, ideas, imaginations, impurities of the mind are in themselves invisible but are communicated to others through look and word and gesture.

What is important is not that a person eats only ritually pure food but that he or she has a clean heart. For it is only in a clean heart that the Holy Spirit can dwell.

> Cleanse, thou refining Flame, all that is mine;
> Self only may remain if thou refine.
> Fix the intention sure, make my desire secure,
> With love my heart keep pure, rooted in thee.
> *Leslie Taylor-Hunt*

Faithlessness Immobilises Us

' "You have so little faith. I tell you the truth, if you have faith as small as a mustard seed, you can say to this mountain, 'Move from here to there' and it will move. Nothing will be impossible for you" '
(vv. 20, 21).

The Christ took time to rebuke his disciples when, because of their lack of faith, they could do nothing for a young boy who suffered from seizures. This particular case was recognised by the Healer as demon possession. The distress, not to say anger, this helplessness caused Jesus was down to the weakness of his team, which unnecessarily prolonged the child's suffering.

' "How long shall I stay with you? How long shall I put up with you?" ' asked Jesus (v. 17). He had hoped for better than this from his disciples after their long apprenticeship with him. Jesus then rebuked the demon and 'it came out of the boy, and he was healed from that moment' (v. 18).

The disciples, in private, asked their Leader, ' "Why couldn't we drive it out?" ' (v. 19). Their Leader's answer was clear: ' "Because you have so little faith" ' (v. 20).

Despite the huge advances in medical knowledge since those days, Jesus' words still have much to say to us. For example, low self-esteem is a contributing factor in many situations, such as sexual abuse, self-harming and depression. The Christian faith offers an antidote to low self-esteem, and every Christian shares the responsibility to make this known. In this regard, is the Christ still disappointed because of the lack of faith of so many of his twenty-first-century disciples?

Perhaps we who baulk at the task of moving mountains should say to our Lord the same words spoken by this young boy's father: ' "I do believe; help me overcome my unbelief!" ' (Mark 9:24).

> Faith, mighty faith, the promise sees
> And looks to that alone;
> Laughs at impossibilities
> And cries: It shall be done!

What About the Children?

....

' "See that you do not look down on one of these little ones.
For I tell you that their angels in heaven always see the face
of my Father in heaven" ' (v. 10).

The angels, we are told, keep their eyes on the face of God the Father and also look after their allocated children. I don't think our angels abandon us when we grow older. We remain God's children. Do we not still need guidance and protection?

Odd Angels

I know I have your angels still
Who resolutely do your will
In oddest places.
Though most of them are well disguised,
With vision Spirit-sensitised,
I know their faces!
They scold, they guide, they comfort me,
They see the danger I don't see
And stop me falling.
Protectors, guardians, seers wise,
With list'ning ears and seeing eyes,
They keep their calling.
Not ethereal and evanescent,
But earthy, warm and ever present;
Odd angels, strangely human-faced,
Strategically, divinely placed,
Are ev'rywhere. I'm grateful!

Who is the Greatest?

'At that time the disciples came to Jesus and asked, "Who is the greatest in the kingdom of heaven?" He called a little child and had him stand among them' (vv. 1, 2).

With the innocent child in the middle of his disciples it was hardly necessary for the Lord to say any more. The greatest of us is the most humble. The one who places himself at the back of the queue, seeking nothing for himself, comes first in God's eyes, though he is unaware of that. If we do not live lives of unconscious holiness we will never enter the kingdom of heaven. What a pity that it can take a whole lifetime to regain the innocent simplicity we were born with!

Luke's Gospel provides details Matthew leaves out, telling us: 'An argument started among the disciples as to which of them would be the greatest. Jesus, knowing their thoughts, took a little child and made him stand beside him' (Luke 9:46, 47). Says Jesus: '"He who is least among you all – he is the greatest"' (v. 48).

It was surely not by accident that Jesus chose a *little* child. Wordsworth suggests that 'shades of the prison house' too early spoil what was once all beauty. The world taints and eventually distorts the most lovely with the suggestion that a bigger house, a more expensive car or success in business are things worth pursuing whatever the cost. It's a lie. Such ambitions demean and impoverish us.

Those who belong to the Church of Christ should not think themselves immune to the disease of wanting to be greatest. I recall a story telling how the devils had no success with a certain holy hermit who indeed seemed immune to all temptation. In despair his demonic attackers appealed to Satan himself to advise them. 'It's not difficult,' he replied. 'Just tell him his younger brother has been elevated to be Bishop of Alexandra. That will finish him!' It did.

To ponder:
Jesus said to them: 'Many who are first will be last, and many who are last will be first.'

(Matthew 19:30)

Child Protection

* *

'"Woe to the world because of the things that cause people to sin!
Such things must come, but woe to the man through
whom they come!"' (v. 7).

When it comes to protecting young people we must do the seemingly impossible. They are so vulnerable to the opinions of their peers and to a hundred other influences, many of them malign. Many people want to make money from our children through the abuse of drink, drugs and sex, and if innocent young people are corrupted along the way that seems to be of little concern. In fact we could be forgiven for thinking that is sometimes the aim. And on only a little less serious level, there are parents and others who see nothing wrong in encouraging children to miss school or make poor career and lifestyle choices.

It's likely that when Jesus spoke of children he was thinking also of fragile and weak adults who are easily misled. We can't dodge our responsibilities for those incapable of accepting responsibility for themselves. Compassion is what Jesus expects of his followers, and when we display it we are doing so to Christ himself. 'Whoever welcomes a little child like this in my name welcomes me,' he tells us (v. 5).

Protecting children from evil influences is good, but not enough. We must introduce them to such principles as honesty, integrity, voluntary service and compassion for the less fortunate.

The eternal consequences of leading young people astray are dire. Says Jesus: '"If anyone causes one of these little ones who believe in me to sin, it would be better for him to have a large millstone hung around his neck and to be drowned in the depths of the sea"' (v. 6). We can't say we haven't been warned!

* *

Little children, little children
Who love their redeemer,
Are his jewels, precious jewels,
His loved and his own.
                    William Orcutt Cushing

Not One Must Be Lost

'"In the same way your Father in heaven is not willing that any of these little ones should be lost"' (v. 14).

Christ's parable of the lost sheep and the shepherd's passion to recover it is one of the best-known stories Jesus told. The tale of the shepherd who seeks until he finds softens the hardest heart. The average person might think it acceptable to lose just 1 per cent of the flock but to the shepherd every one of his sheep is precious – however prone to wandering they might be.

Jesus clearly knew about sheep and shepherds. When he claimed that the Father-God is the super-shepherd he had the right to do so, because he shares the Father's shepherd-heart. He was talking from that heart when he told how the true shepherd seeks for as long as it takes to find the missing member of his flock. And we should believe him when he says: '"If he finds it, I tell you the truth, he is happier about that one sheep than about the ninety-nine that did not wander off"' (v. 13).

Every Christian must be a tireless seeker of the lost. This is not an optional matter. Says Jesus: '"In the same way your Father in heaven is not willing that any of these little ones should be lost"' (v. 14). And we, too, should be 'not willing'.

Sadly, in many churches the proportion of the flock who go missing is much more than 1 per cent. How should we pray for them? Persistently!

The king of love my Shepherd is,
Whose goodness faileth never;
I nothing lack if I am his
And he is mine forever.
Perverse and foolish oft I strayed,
But yet in love he sought me,
And on his shoulder gently laid
And home rejoicing brought me.
Henry Williams Baker

The Value of the Group

'"If your brother sins against you, go and show him his fault, just between the two of you. If he listens to you, you have won your brother over. But if he will not listen, take one or two others along, so that 'every matter may be established by the testimony of two or three witnesses'"' (vv. 15, 16).

It's interesting that Jesus established a system to solve disagreement among the disciples. Two brothers in Christ who disagree should attempt to resolve the issue between themselves. If they fail, one or two others should mediate. If that attempt also fails, the matter should be presented to the whole church for a decision. If there is still no resolution the one at fault should leave the congregation.

It's not a perfect system but it prevents just one person from acting as judge and jury. The likelihood of a miscarriage of justice is minimised when a group decision is required.

Jesus says unanimity is also important when it comes to prayer. 'I tell you,' he said, 'that if two of you on earth agree about anything you ask for, it will be done for you by my Father in heaven' (v. 19).

These words, and those that follow, set down three principles. The size of the agreeing group need not be large; just two or three is enough. They must come together in Christ's name, not their own. Christ will then be with them in Spirit.

Like it or not, the Church has to spend some time in administration, including, sadly, sorting out problems between members. More happily, not only has Jesus given us a plan, he's also given us a promise: '"Where two or three come together in my name, there am I with them"' (v. 20). With him involved we won't go far wrong.

To ponder:
When we meet with other Christians we sometimes sing: 'Here, Lord, assembled in thy name thy work to do, thy help we claim.' Let's remember that claiming help is always a good idea . . . not least when we have to witness alone.

No Mercy for the Merciless

*'Peter came to Jesus and asked, "Lord, how many times shall
I forgive my brother when he sins against me? Up to seven times?"
Jesus answered, "I tell you, not seven times but seventy-seven times"'*
(vv. 21, 22).

Our Lord promises that penitents may count on his pardon however monstrous their mistakes and sins. He made it clear to Peter that there are no boundaries to his absolution. Peter must have been glad to recall those words when his weakness was laid bare before the Saviour he had sworn never to betray. Peter's bitter tears of regret (see Matthew 26:75) were proof enough of his repentance.

The parable told here by Jesus is one we need to read often. The warning it contains needs to be noted: those who wish for mercy must show mercy to others. Our refusal to forgive disqualifies us from receiving forgiveness. Our withholding of pardon to others shows we know nothing about the experience. How dare we ask for it?

Once, leaving an evangelical rally, Bramwell Booth – second General of The Salvation Army – was besieged by a crowd of people. They wanted him to sign a plea seeking a reprieve for a criminal who had been condemned to hang. Booth's companion explained there was otherwise no hope for the man. 'It's a matter of mercy, then?' said Bramwell Booth, reaching for the pen held out to him. 'We all need mercy. All of us!'

I like Charles Wesley's hymn:

> Depth of mercy! Can there be
> Mercy still reserved for me?
> Can my God his wrath forbear?
> Me, the chief of sinners, spare?

Yes, God will have mercy on us. So long as we show mercy to others.

A *prayer:*
'God be merciful to me a sinner.'

(Luke 18:13, KJV)

What Do We Get out of It?

' "I tell you the truth, it is hard for a rich man to enter the kingdom of heaven. Again I tell you, it is easier for a camel to go through the eye of a needle than for a rich man to enter the kingdom of God" ' (vv. 23, 24).

A few days ago we read how hard the disciples of Jesus found it to ignore the question of status (Matthew 18:1-4). When Jesus saw the sons of Zebedee arguing about which of them would have the highest place, he had to put them right and tell them that true greatness comes from serving others (see Mark 10:35-45).

Our Lord must have been disappointed to have to address the same issue with Peter – the disciple who had so much influence on the others – when he wondered what he might expect in return for the troubles he had faced. 'We have left everything to follow you! What then will there be for us?' Peter asked (Matthew 19:27). In Peter's mind, the disciples had nothing more to sacrifice. They had already left everything to follow Jesus. Surely that counted for something!

The Christ gently called his disciples to focus on spiritual matters rather than worldly things. We are not to have illusions about greatness or try to keep our spiritual account 'in credit' by anything we do. 'Many who are first will be last, and many who are last will be first,' warned Jesus (v. 30).

If I ever met a great lady it was Violet, who lived in Manchester, in the north of England. Of great age, she was the epitome of humility. Among other things she sold Salvation Army publications in a dozen public houses every week. When I accompanied her the customers treated me with respect. But they adored and revered Violet. They recognised her humble witness as greatness.

People notice these things. We might fool ourselves with feelings of self-importance but others are less easily taken in. And God never is.

A prayer:
Lord, help us to be as good as some people think we are. Or, at least, willing to try to be!

Joy among the Angels

' "I tell you, there is rejoicing in the presence of the angels of God over one sinner who repents" ' (v. 10).

I reckon we should read the story of the prodigal son at least twice a year . . . and also on every occasion when we feel the need to repent after joining the prodigals' ranks!

Another Prodigal

Not always wise, I run away from truth;
Welcome the false like any foolish youth,
And in no time regret my falls and fears;
Hide my mistakes and try to dry my tears.
Ashamed, in prayer, nothing else can I do.
Nothing to say, I make my way to you;
Back to my home, back to your love, your pain,
I have the cheek to slip back in again!
Your elder sons can make no sense of this:
The shoes, the ring, the pardon and the kiss.
Thank you that I find things still the same:
Love is your nature and Love your name!

Best Boys?

....

'The mother of Zebedee's sons came to Jesus with her sons and,
kneeling down, asked a favour of him . . . . She said, "Grant that
one of these two sons of mine may sit at your right and the other
at your left in your kingdom"' (vv. 20, 21).

It's hardly surprising that Jesus told this mother who was so
ambitious for her sons, '"You don't know what you're asking"' (v. 22).
Little did she know that the cup they would have to drink from would
not be sweet. Mothers generally have high hopes for their children but,
given that there could be only two seats next to the throne in Christ's
kingdom, what she was asking was excessive, to say the least. What
about the sons of other mothers? No wonder we read: 'When the ten
heard about this, they were indignant with the two brothers' (v. 24).

Some parents are not altogether selfless when they dream of high
rewards for their children. Their boasting and pride suggests they want
something for themselves from their children's success. As a result,
some children are pushed beyond their capacities, with catastrophic
results. It is not unknown for children who fail to reach their parents'
high expectations to take their own lives. Concern at this mother's
unrealistic demands was surely behind Jesus' seemingly unsym-
pathetic response.

What can we legitimately dream for our children and ourselves? I
believe all the children of God are called to be the best they can be. But
if we seek to be great, it should be greatness in service and selflessness
and humility – as modelled for us by our Servant-King, Jesus, who said:
'"Whoever wants to become great among you must be your servant"'
(v. 26).

The following verse should be our prayer. Even if advancing years
makes the word 'young' inappropriate, it is a worthy ambition:

> Just as I am, young, strong and free,
> To be the best that I can be
> For truth and righteousness and thee,
> Lord of my life, I come.
>   *Marianne Farningham*

No Lording It

Jesus called them together and said, "You know that the rulers of the Gentiles lord it over them, and their high officials exercise authority over them. Not so with you"' (v. 25).

I wonder if Jesus meant his statement to be taken as a question: 'It's not like that among you . . . is it?' He himself never lorded it over anyone. He ate with the unacceptable. He touched lepers. He washed his disciples' feet. Even when he was dying he spoke kindly to the thief who was being crucified alongside him. He did not strut around or expect to be waited on. He reminded his followers that he came to serve, not to be served.

In today's society people often act according to their status. Christ was not like that, and as his followers we should follow his example.

Little things are important. When I was a cadet in training for Salvation Army officership my college principal played the piano magnificently – but not in front of us. Even when a new piano was presented to the college and the donor asked him to be the first person to play it publicly he chose to play a simple melody with no frills. Nothing could persuade him to show off! He was a true follower of Christ with genuine humility, and he made humility beautiful to us.

Jesus asked: '"Who is greater, the one who is at the table or the one who serves? Is it not the one who is at the table? But I am among you as one who serves"' (Luke 22:27).

It is not easy to be a Christian. We not only have to know Christ, we have to be like him. Perhaps that's why few churches have long queues outside their front doors!

A prayer:

> Teach, O teach us, holy Child,
> By thy face so meek and mild,
> Teach us to resemble thee
> In thy sweet humility.
> *Edward Caswall*

Buying and Selling

....

*Jesus entered the temple area and drove out all who were buying and
selling there. He overturned the tables of the money-changers and the
benches of those selling doves' (v. 12).*

It's hard to imagine Jesus in the Temple with a whip in his hand.
John's Gospel tells us it was a self-made whip of cord, possibly more
symbolic than effective (John 2:15). However, his voice and his
gestures were probably enough to drive out the sheep, doves and
angry-faced traders.

The Outer Court was the only part of the temple where Gentiles
could go for prayer and meditation, but seekers after truth had to
compete with the cries of the marketplace. Worse still, the traders were
what today would be described as rip-off merchants. The only animals
which could be sacrificed in the Temple were those bought there, so
they were sold to pilgrims at hugely inflated prices. And the money-
changers similarly profited by their privileged position, charging
extravagant exchange rates for the Temple money which had to be
used there.

Jesus had no time for this. They were robbers, he said (v. 13). His
reference to Isaiah 56:7 and Jeremiah 7:11 must have stung them: ' "It
is written," he said to them, "'My house will be called a house of
prayer', but you are making it a 'den of robbers'." '

Happier moments followed when Jesus healed the blind and lame in
the Temple. The Hebrew word 'Hosanna' is often translated as 'Save!'
but more accurately it means 'Praise!' The crowds were singing 'Praise
the Son of David!' recognising that Jesus came from the royal house of
King David. When the children chanted the same words the chief
priests and teachers of the law were indignant: 'Do you hear what
these children are saying?' they asked him (v. 16).

Jesus always seemed to find time for the children. If we do the same
we shall win his approval. His response to the angry priests and
scholars made reference to Psalm 8:2: 'Have you never read, "'From
the lips of children and infants you have ordained praise'"'?

Yes, they had read it. But they had not understood.

Second Thoughts

'"What do you think? There was a man who had two sons. He went to the first and said, 'Son, go and work today in the vineyard.' 'I will not,' he answered, but later he changed his mind and went"' (vv. 28, 29).

Sir Winston Churchill is supposed to have said, 'Never apologise, never explain!' But he did change his mind occasionally. If he had been incapable of second thoughts he would have been a less-great man and less useful to his country. It wasn't easy to persuade him to rethink something but he could be persuaded, by the wife he loved, to do so, and when he did it was usually for the good.

In a parable, Jesus tells us of two sons, very different in nature. The first was unhelpful. His immediate rejection of a request for help from his father consisted of just three short words: 'I will not' (v. 29). Surely his father did not deserve such short shrift. But then that son had second thoughts. He changed his mind and did as his father asked. The Church would be significantly stronger if some of us Christians changed our minds and gave more readily of our time, talents and comparative riches to the cause of Christ.

The second son immediately said 'yes' to the same plea but failed to keep his word. He answered, 'I will, sir,' but he didn't do as he promised (v. 30). Unreliable people are the bane of our life. We would rather do the job ourselves. It would be a different world if all the disciples of Jesus kept their promises.

Is that what this story means? The listening crowds understood that the Christ preferred the son who at least eventually did as he was asked. Is there a warning here for us?

Should there not be a third son in the parable? One who would say 'yes' at once and keep his promise cheerfully? Second thoughts are better than a continuing refusal, but it's even better if no repentance is needed. Can the Master rely on me?

To ponder:
'Mine to rise when thou dost call me, Lifelong though the journey be.'

Susie Forrest Swift

Dishonest Tenant

'When the harvest time approached, he sent his servants to the tenants to collect his fruit. The tenants seized his servants; they beat one, killed another, and stoned a third' (vv. 34, 35).

Here we find Jesus issuing a warning about the danger of forgetting that we are tenants, not landlords. God is Lord of all. Everything belongs to him. Our responsibility is to be good stewards of what God provides for our needs and enjoyment.

When tenants act as if they own what has been provided for them, problems are inevitable. We see that on a global scale when people and nations act as if the world – or at least the part of it they occupy – belongs to them and can be treated as they like. Our responsibility to act as 'tenants' – stewards rather than owners – of God's creation is implicit in the words of Jesus: ' "Why do you call me, 'Lord, Lord,' and do not do what I say?" ' (Luke 6:46). I fear he must ask the question still.

The weaknesses of Christendom today have much to do with our habit of ignoring Jesus' teaching. Matthew 21:45 tells us: 'When the chief priests and the Pharisees heard Jesus' parables, they knew he was talking about them.' At least they recognised themselves. Too often we assume that the unflattering comment we hear is addressed to anyone but us!

Said Jesus: ' "I tell you that the kingdom of God will be taken away from you and given to a people who will produce its fruit" ' (v. 43). Churches that are not bearing fruit should urgently discover why that is. And do something about it!

> All good gifts around us
> Are sent from heaven above;
> Then thank the Lord, O thank the Lord
> For all his love!
>
> *Matthias Claudius*

Preaching Without Practice

'"But do not do what they do, for they do not practise what they preach. They tie up heavy loads and put them on men's shoulders, but they themselves are not willing to lift a finger to move them"' (vv, 3, 4).

I don't believe Jesus took any pleasure in condemning the outlook and actions of the Pharisees and teachers of the law who were so often the subject of his criticism. He saw them as poor examples to the students who sat at their feet, and he told them so. But they surely aroused sadness in him as well as anger. How had the spiritual leaders of the children of God so lost their way? He had to warn those who looked to them for the truth that these men did not practise what they preached (v. 3).

All who today speak on behalf of Christianity – if only by their daily living – should heed Christ's condemnatory words. If the way we live is not in harmony with the teaching we present then we are worse than fruitless, we are enemies of the gospel. The observer wants not only to hear something beautiful but also to see something beautiful. None of us is perfect but onlookers should be able to see Christ in what we do as well as what we say.

There is little worse than a communicator with a beautiful voice, rich vocabulary and charming face – but a phoney experience. Stammering, almost inarticulate but authentic and sincere deliverers of the truth are what is needed in Christ's service. The inauthentic who hide behind masks of sincerity are always revealed for what they are, sooner or later.

Jesus warns us against pretence. He suggests that counterfeit teachers can often be recognised by their habit of insisting on impossible standards from their students while never themselves achieving – or perhaps even attempting – those heights of perfection. As Jesus puts it, '"They themselves are not willing to lift a finger"' (v. 4).

Jesus says such people love to be noticed and acknowledged and praised. '"Everything they do is done for men to see,"' he observes (v. 5). Let's look and learn, and so avoid the trap of artificiality and hypocrisy!

Sit Down!

* *

'"People will come from east and west and north and south,
and will take their places at the feast in the kingdom of God.
Indeed there are those who are last who will be first, and first
who will be last"' (vv 29, 30).

Some things that seem to matter a lot in this life – our status, our wealth, our skin colour, our education – will matter not a jot in eternity. Praise God!

Thy Kingdom Come

They shall come from the east, they shall come from the west,
And sit down in the kingdom of God;
Both the rich and the poor, the despised, the distressed,
They'll sit down in the kingdom of God.
And none will ask what they have been,
Provided that their robes are clean;
They shall come from the east, they shall come from the west,
And sit down in the kingdom of God.
They shall come from the east, they shall come from the west,
And sit down in the kingdom of God;
To be met by their Father and welcomed and blessed,
And sit down in the kingdom of God.
The black, the white, the dark, the fair,
Your colour will not matter there;
They shall come from the east, they will come from the west,
And sit down in the kingdom of God.
They shall come from the east, they shall come from the west,
And sit down in the kingdom of God;
Out of great tribulation to triumph and rest,
They'll sit down in the kingdom of God.
From every tribe and every race,
All men as brothers shall embrace;
They shall come from the east, they shall come from the west,
And sit down in the kingdom of God.

Gnats and Camels

● ●

'"You give a tenth of your spices – mint, dill and cummin. But you have neglected the more important matters of the law – justice, mercy and faithfulness"' (v. 23).

It's not surprising that the *New International Version* heads the twenty-third chapter of Matthew with the words 'Seven Woes'. The unhappiness of Christ with the teachers of the law and the Pharisees is clear from what he says about them. Again and again he calls them hypocrites. If there was one thing the Son of Man could not bear it was the hypocrisy of those who only pretended to be servants of God. When he pointed his finger in their direction it was to encourage his disciples to be nothing like them.

Jesus paints two pictures in words to make his criticisms plain. In the first we see these impeccably dressed Pharisees and men of great learning making a show of the way they measure out what they give to God. Look at the care with which they give exactly one tenth (and not a grain more) of their valuable spices, while justice, mercy and faithfulness are given no attention at all.

Now look at these proud know-alls carefully drinking their soup, covering the bowl with white muslin to prevent it becoming ritually impure through contact with tiny gnats. But – metaphorically – when their backs are turned a camel falls into the bowl and they swallow it unknowingly. The crowd surely laughed, but was Jesus smiling? I think not. What is sadder than a proclaimed servant of God giving all his attention to things of little importance while, in the meantime, justice is not done, mercy is not offered and the faithful are not recognised?

We're all guilty sometimes of neglecting significant things while making a song and dance about something of no real importance. Lord, help us keep our priorities in order!

....

To ponder:
'Seek first his kingdom and his righteousness.'

(Matthew 6:33)

The Tears of God

••

'"How often I have longed to gather your children together, as a hen gathers her chicks under her wings, but you were not willing"' (v. 37).

The Son of God owed nothing to the people of Jerusalem. They had killed the prophets God sent them and stoned his messengers. Yet Jesus tells them he had *often* longed to gather them together and protect them as a mother hen protects her chicks.

How telling that word 'often' is! Not just once or twice, but *often* the compassionate Son of God tried to protect the people he loved from the disaster on which they seemed set. Verse 37 is a heartbreaking lament which reveals how close God is to shedding tears over his unappreciative children.

One of the saddest phrases in the Bible is the statement of Jesus to the people of Jerusalem: 'But you were not willing!' Can the designs of the Almighty really be thwarted by ordinary human beings? The *New English Bible* translation says: 'But you would not let me!' The result? God warns: '"I tell you, you will not see me again until you say, 'Blessed is he who comes in the name of the Lord'"' (v. 39). For the people of Jerusalem, it's a self-inflicted wound.

But before we become too critical, how often do we thwart God's plans for us? What could he do for us if we allowed him free rein? How often do we move the Christ to tears through our stubbornness?

••

> As the bird beneath her feathers
> Guards the objects of her care,
> So the Lord his children gathers,
> Spreads his wings, and hides us there;
> Thus protected,
> All our foes we boldly dare.
>
> *Thomas Kelly*

Be Prepared

....

'"At that time the kingdom of heaven will be like ten virgins who took their lamps and went out to meet the bridegroom. Five of them were foolish and five were wise. The foolish ones took their lamps but did not take any oil with them"' (vv. 1–3).

We've been considering some of the warnings issued by the Master. The story of the bridesmaids with their lamps is a cautionary tale we do well to remember. I wonder if General Robert Baden-Powell, founder of the Scouting movement, took his movement's motto – 'Be Prepared' – from this parable. We cannot predict what circumstances will face us day by day but the servants of God are to be ready for every disaster and every opportunity.

When I was a lad my parents were Salvation Army officers in Whitehaven, Cumbria. It was a mining area and one day a pit disaster led to the deaths of more than a hundred miners. Prior to officership, my father had been a miner for twelve years and this was not the first time he had been involved in the like of this. He visited the homes of every bereaved family. He knew how to talk and when to listen. In the tragedy he saw an opportunity for serving the suffering and he was ready for it. Years later he returned to Whitehaven to retire and people there had not forgotten him.

If we Christians are to have anything to offer at such times perhaps we should all equip ourselves for one ministry or another: listening, understanding, comforting, encouraging, equipping. In such ways do people enter the kingdom, and in such ways the kingdom grows.

But not every opportunity announces itself in advance. 'Keep watch,' says Jesus, 'because you do not know the day or the hour' (v. 13).

....

To ponder:
'Look busy,' says the car bumper sticker, 'Jesus is coming again.' Don't let's kid ourselves that he'll be that easily fooled!

Kings of all Kinds

Introduction

The kings we are examining this month are far from perfect. The writer of these chapters of Scripture gives good marks to one or two monarchs, but they are the exceptions. When things were difficult, those called to lead often failed their people. Sometimes this was down to their passion for popularity. Sometimes they listened to foolish council. Most often, the kings strayed to other gods simply because they could not bring themselves to trust enough in the true God. They thought two (or more!) gods were better than one, despite all the advice they received to the contrary.

But before we twenty-first-century Christians condemn their weakness, let's remember we sometimes do little better. Jesus told us clearly that we cannot serve God and 'mammon' – the world. But sometimes we try to. Happily, some of the kings ultimately listened to the Lord's prophets and recalled God's children to the ways of truth and righteousness. So many years later, we can still learn from their stories.

He is not King
Till we give him his kingdom;
He has no throne
Until we give up ours.
Unless we make him room,
The Christ is homeless.
Unless we let him reign
He has few powers.

He is not truly King
Until we crown him
Lord of all we have,
Our hopes, our schemes.
And then our ugliness
Is touched with beauty
And loveliness beyond
Our wildest dreams!

Two Candidates

....

' "What is it you want?" the king asked. She said to him, "My lord, you
yourself swore to me your servant by the LORD your God: 'Solomon
your son shall become king after me, and he will sit on my throne.'
But now Adonijah has become king, and you, my lord the king,
do not know about it" ' (vv. 16–18).

King David was dying. His son Adonijah, aged about thirty-five, and his favourite son, twenty-year-old Solomon, were both candidates for the succession. Although David had the right to choose who should be the next king, ambitious Adonijah declared himself the new sovereign without David's knowledge.

The prophet Nathan told Bathsheba, Solomon's mother, to inform the king. Fearful of the treatment she and Solomon would receive from Adonijah, Bathsheba told David something had to be done: ' "Otherwise, as soon as my lord the king is laid to rest with his fathers, I and my son Solomon will be treated as criminals" ' (v. 21). She was right.

There's nothing new under the sun, some might say. Leadership struggles take place in every land, in every generation. Some involve military coups, others merely 'dirty tricks' in the political arena. In the time of Solomon, the competitors were more than likely to slaughter each other.

The supporters of King David moved quickly at his instructions. Solomon was immediately declared king. His head was anointed with oil, 'They sounded the trumpet and all the people shouted, "Long live King Solomon!" And all the people went up after him, playing flutes and rejoicing greatly, so that the ground shook with the sound' (vv. 39, 40).

The supporters of Adonijah took the news to their leader: ' "Our lord King David has made Solomon king . . . Solomon has taken his seat on the royal throne. Also, the royal officials have come to congratulate our lord King David" ' (vv. 43, 46, 47).

Would there be any mercy for the older brother? In a similar situation today, how do we treat our rivals?

A Cry for Mercy

....

'Adonijah, in fear of Solomon, went and took hold of the horns of the altar. Then Solomon was told, "Adonijah is afraid of King Solomon and is clinging to the horns of the altar"' (vv. 50, 51).

The horns which ornamented the corners of the altar had great importance. Someone whose life was in danger could cling to the horns and plead for protection. The cry for mercy would at least be considered. In this case Solomon was compassionate and said, ' "If he shows himself to be a worthy man, not a hair of his head will fall to the ground; but if evil is found in him, he will die"' (v. 52). Adonijah was released and sent home. He would be safe, at least while King David was alive.

We remember that David's character and record were not without blemish. He had arranged for the death of the husband of Bathsheba so that she could be one of his wives. Nathan the prophet rebuked the king for his crimes of adultery and murder, both punishable by death. David confessed his sins and was forgiven (2 Samuel 11 and 12).

Years later, when David was dying, he gave the names of those who had offended him to Solomon, with instructions for them to be killed. We might have hoped that a king who had himself received pardon would have given it to others on his deathbed, if not before. But for Adonijah, this time there was no mercy. No doubt still hoping to become king himself, he asked if he might be given David's wife Abishag to be his own bride. Solomon was angry. ' "Adonijah shall be put to death today!"' (2:24). And he was.

Such behaviour was thought acceptable at the time. The world had much to learn about mercy. No wonder Jesus declared centuries later that he had come to be 'the light of the world' (John 8:12). If followed, his teaching – ' "I tell you who hear me: Love your enemies, do good to those who hate you, bless those who curse you"' (Luke 6:27) – would result in an end to darkness. But forgiveness is a personal choice and not everyone manages it. Mercy can still be in short supply.

Making Progress

••

'"Now, O Lord my God, you have made your servant king in place of my father David. But I am only a little child and do not know how to carry out my duties . . . So give your servant a discerning heart to govern your people" . . . The Lord was pleased that Solomon had asked for this' (vv. 7, 9, 10).

Solomon was a young man but wise enough to ask the Almighty to give him wisdom. That showed humility as well as discernment. He wanted to be able to distinguish between right and wrong and asked for a heart to govern his fellow countrymen and women as God's people, not his own.

Solomon described himself as a servant-king. Had he learnt that from his father David? Dictator-kings abounded, servant-kings were rare. Today, presidents and prime ministers sometimes talk of servant leadership but rarely demonstrate it. And others in less exalted positions often do no better. The leader of a hugely populated country and the office manager responsible for just a handful of staff both need to be 'servants'. Too many are bullies. In the Church, too, servant-leaders are seriously needed.

The things we ask for reveal a great deal about us. God was pleased with Solomon's request. He might have asked for popularity or gold. But he asked for wisdom and was given it. God's pleasure is seen in his words: '"In your lifetime you will have no equal among kings"' (v. 13). That was no false promise and no exaggeration. The wisdom of Solomon is a legend we still talk about. His dream was fulfilled because he kept the conditions that went with God's gift of wisdom: he walked in God's ways and obeyed God's commands.

William Booth, founder of The Salvation Army, once said: 'The tendency of fire is to go out.' Solomon kept his promises. Long may we do the same!

••

Ye servants of God, your Master proclaim,
And publish abroad his wonderful name;
The name all-victorious of Jesus extol;
His Kingdom is glorious and rules over all.
Charles Wesley

Chosen

••

'"You did not choose me, but I chose you and appointed you to go and bear fruit – fruit that will last"' (v. 16).

The twelve disciples were not the only people called by God to serve him. Every Christian is called to ministry of some kind. Each of us is chosen too!

You Have Chosen Me

You have chosen me; I have heard your call.
I'll take up my cross, and I'll give you all.
I know you'll supply everything I lack
If I follow you, holding nothing back.

You have chosen me? Then I shall not fear.
When I need you most, I shall know you're near.
And your will for me is your own affair;
While I walk your way I am in your care!

You have chosen me, though it seems absurd,
To protect the poor, to proclaim your word.
Your ambassador to this world below,
Where you choose to send, I'll be glad to go!

You have chosen me? Then I dare not ask
To be reassigned to a lesser task.
When the way is dark and I cannot see,
I'll remember then, you have chosen me!

Wisdom at Work

* *

'The woman whose son was alive was filled with compassion for her
son and said to the king, "Please, my lord, give her the living baby!
Don't kill him!" But the other said: "Neither I nor you shall have him.
Cut him in two!"' (v. 26).

This is a memorable story about the wisdom of Solomon. Many people know it well. The babies were the children of two prostitutes, so it's possible the identity of both fathers was unknown. But clearly the children were of importance to the mothers, as both claimed the surviving child. The mothers may once have been friends, as they shared the same house, but that friendship was not enough to guarantee truth from at least one of them. For one was clearly lying to Solomon. Notice how he determined which one.

Solomon had many wives and children. He knew from experience that a mother will always do what is best for her child, whatever the personal cost. In the concentration camps of the Second World War it was not unknown for a mother to give her child to a stranger if it meant the child's life might be saved. And earlier in the Old Testament we have the example of the mother of Moses, who risked her precious son to the waters in a fragile basket in a risky attempt to save his life.

Solomon's wisdom paid off. The lying mother revealed her identity through her lack of love. As hymnwriter Joseph Buck declared: 'Love has a language, all its own making.' It 'stands the test'.

What language do we speak day by day? Are our words and our actions clearly interpreted as love? Or, like the bogus mother, do we reveal the inauthenticity of our faith by our readiness to compromise?

* *

> Love's life is always all its best giving,
> Giving, it lives, for love thrives on this;
> Thus, when the best in this world is decaying,
> Love will live on, for love stands the test.
>
> *Joseph Buck*

Successful Solomon

'The people of Judah and Israel were as numerous as the sand on the seashore; they ate, they drank and they were happy . . . During Solomon's lifetime Judah and Israel, from Dan to Beersheba, lived in safety, each man under his own vine and fig tree' (vv. 20, 25).

The rapidity of Solomon's success was staggering. He married the Pharaoh's daughter, making an ally of Egypt. The neighbouring countries were his subjects and paid tribute to him. The first twenty verses of 1 Kings 4 reveal his success in matters of organisation and administration. The king was short of nothing. Verse 26 tells us: 'Solomon had four thousand stalls for chariot horses, and twelve thousand horses.'

His wisdom was legendary even in his youth: 'God gave Solomon wisdom and very great insight, and a breadth of understanding as measureless as the sand on the seashore' (v. 29). He was an educated man, too, and a literate one: 'He spoke three thousand proverbs and his songs numbered a thousand and five' (v. 32). We can read some of his writings in the book of Proverbs. We are told that 'men of all nations came to listen to Solomon's wisdom' (v. 34).

Solomon had many interests but his first passion was the building of the Temple which his father had only dreamt of. He planned a magnificent palace for himself, too – but the Temple would come first. A truly wise man has his priorities in the right order.

Hiram, king of Tyre, was just one who recognised Solomon's greatness: ' "Praise be to the LORD today, for he has given David a wise son to rule over this great nation" ' (5:7). May the way we live today lead others to rejoice and give the praise to God!

I often say my prayers; but do I ever pray?
And do the wishes of my heart go with the words I say?
I may as well kneel down and worship gods of stone,
As offer to the living God a prayer of words alone.
                                        Annie Sherwood Hawks

Nothing was Spared

··

*'The word of the LORD came to Solomon: "As for this temple you are
building, if you follow my decrees, carry out my regulations and keep
all my commands and obey them, I will fulfil through you the promise
I gave to David your father. And I will live among the Israelites and
will not abandon my people Israel" ' (vv. 11–13).*

Many people helped build the Temple. The craftsmen of Hiram and
Gebal made their contribution along with the Israelites. And
there were 3,300 supervisors. Scripture often talks of Solomon building
the Temple – but he didn't do it on his own! Solomon's greatest contribution was listening to the word of the Lord and obeying. There would
have been no success without Israel's continuing obedience to God's
commands.

Out of respect for the Almighty, the noise of the building work was
kept to a minimum: 'Only blocks dressed at the quarry were used, and
no hammer, chisel or any other iron tool was heard at the temple site
while it was being built' (v. 7).

No expense was spared, and that was particularly true of the
Temple's inner sanctuary, the Most Holy Place. Everything was
covered with pure gold, especially the Ark of the Covenant, into which
the stone tablets bearing the Ten Commandments were placed. The
gold-covered twin cherubs whose wings spread protectively over the
ark must alone have been one of the wonders of the world.

Christians who today worship in simple, largely unadorned and
practical premises might feel the whole enterprise was a gross extra-
vagance, but the goal of Solomon and his people was to bring glory to
God. Different priorities today may well be justified, so long as our
different ways of worshipping and serving the Lord truly please him.
They will if our aim is to glorify God, not ourselves.

···

To ponder:
**William Shakespeare wrote: 'All that glisters is not gold.' Is
everything in our heart's 'most holy place' covered with 'pure
gold'? Our ambitions, our motives, our priorities?**

A Home for the Ark

'The priests took up the ark, and they brought up the ark of the LORD and the Tent of Meeting and all the sacred furnishings in it' (vv. 3, 4).

Solomon's rebuilding of the Temple was almost finished and he turned his attention to the building of his palace. It was a major project. So 1 Kings 7 gives us a detailed description of a magnificent dwelling built with the very best materials and craftsmanship. It included a throne room, a hall of justice and a hall for the daughter of Pharaoh whom he had married. The first verse tells us: 'It took Solomon thirteen years . . . to complete the construction of his palace.'

For many years the Ark of the Covenant had been housed temporarily in Zion, the city of David. The Tent of Meeting (the Tabernacle), with its sacred furnishings, was lodged in Gibeon. All the men of Israel came to King Solomon and accompanied the ark to its future home in the new Temple. Verse 5 tells us that so many sheep and cattle were sacrificed they could not be counted! The priests then carried the ark, containing Moses' two stone tablets, into the Temple's Holy of Holies.

The Israelites believed God was in that place. 'When the priests withdrew from the Holy Place, the cloud filled the temple of the LORD. And the priests could not perform their service because of the cloud, for the glory of the LORD filled his temple' (vv. 10, 11). They all knew the meaning of the cloud. The same thing had happened when God was present in the Tabernacle at Sinai many years before.

Solomon then blessed the people with beautiful prayers of praise (vv. 14–53). These show us how mature the king had become in spiritual things. He talks now about confession and forgiveness. He decrees that there should be a place for foreigners. 'Do whatever the foreigner asks of you,' he told them (v. 43). He had come a long way in his thinking.

Solomon's blessing upon the people declared: '"May the LORD our God be with us as he was with our fathers; may he never leave us nor forsake us. May he turn our hearts to him, to walk in all his ways"' (vv. 57, 58). Thousands of years later we can all say amen to that.

The Queen of Sheba Visits

"In wisdom and wealth you have far exceeded the report I heard" (v. 7).

The visit of the queen of Sheba to Solomon's kingdom is described in chapter 10. The queen expected to see splendid things but what she saw went way beyond her expectations. She was totally dazzled. She posed many questions to her host and was awed by his answers. ' "I did not believe these things until I came and saw with my own eyes. Indeed, not even half was told me; in wisdom and wealth you have far exceeded the report I heard," ' she declared (v. 7).

She and Solomon exchanged hugely valuable gifts: 'Never again were so many spices brought in as those the queen of Sheba gave to King Solomon' (v. 10). But even those gifts were small compared to Solomon's total wealth. His store of gold continued to grow at an undiminished pace: 'The weight of the gold that Solomon received yearly was 666 talents, not including the revenues from the merchants and traders and from all the Arabian kings and the governors of the land' (vv. 14, 15).

Solomon exhibited his wealth with hundreds of gold shields which he displayed in his palace, and he had a great throne made for himself which in splendour outshone anything previously seen: 'The king made a great throne inlaid with ivory and overlaid with fine gold. The throne had six steps, and its back had a rounded top. On both sides of the seat were armrests, with a lion standing beside each of them. Twelve lions stood on the six steps, one at either end of each step. Nothing like it had ever been made for any other kingdom' (vv. 18–20).

However, Solomon's accumulation of chariots and horses was against the law of Moses. It was not a wise move, as we shall see.

To ponder:
To whose glory do we live? God's, or our own? Charles Coller was in no doubt. He wrote: 'To work or to witness, to go or remain, his smile of approval my infinite gain.'

An Unhappy Future

*'As Solomon grew old, his wives turned his heart after other gods,
and his heart was not fully devoted to the LORD his God,
as the heart of David his father had been' (v. 4).*

It might be amusing to say that any king with 700 wives and 300 concubines was looking for trouble! But they did indeed prove problematic. They had no respect for the Temple; instead Solomon established 'high places' – altars – for them to worship at, burning incense and offering sacrifices to their gods. The Almighty's warning was ignored and in the end Solomon was, to a large degree, wooed away from the God of his father and ancestors. God was not pleased and, no doubt sadly, announced that the descendants of David would not continue to inherit the kingdom after Solomon.

We are told: 'The king made silver as common in Jerusalem as stones, and cedar as plentiful as sycamore-fig trees in the foothills' (1 Kings 10:27). But he had lost the most precious thing: pure, obedient faith in the Lord. When he realised this his regret must have been profound.

The Lord raised up adversaries against Solomon; first one, then another (1 Kings 11:14, 23). Then Jeroboam, a man of standing who was one of the king's most favoured officials, rebelled against him (v. 26). Solomon, the most popular of kings, was popular no longer.

The prophet Ahijah met Jeroboam and dramatically tore up his new cloak into twelve pieces, telling Jeroboam that ten pieces of the kingdom would belong to him when Solomon died (vv. 29–31). Solomon did his best to defeat his enemy but Jeroboam fled to the security of the king of Egypt and did not emerge until Solomon died. The brilliant king had reigned for forty years, but his disobedience to God ultimately made him less than he might have been. It's a message for us all.

To ponder:
'What shall it profit a man,' asked Jesus, 'if he shall gain the whole world, and lose his own soul?'

(Mark 8:36, KJV)

The Winds and Waves Obey Him

*'A furious squall came up, and the waves broke over the boat,
so that it was nearly swamped. Jesus was in the stern, sleeping on a
cushion. The disciples woke him and said to him, "Teacher, don't you
care if we drown?" He got up, rebuked the wind and said to the waves,
"Quiet! Be still!" Then the wind died down' (vv. 37–39).*

We've all felt swamped by our problems at some time, and sometimes we've been tempted to feel Jesus has been sleeping through it. Happily, many of us have also experienced his calming powers over the elements threatening us.

The Winds Obeyed!

You spoke, and the winds obeyed you!
You called, and the waters heard!
The storm that sought to sink the ship
Subsided at your word.
You spoke, and the rain-storm faltered.
You called, and the sun came through.
The rainbow hurried to deck the sky
And paint the waters blue!
You speak, and my fears obey you.
You call, and my doubts are stilled.
My empty, aching, hurting soul
With peace and calm is filled.
You speak and my faith is firmer.
You call and my hopes grow strong.
Your presence scatters the darkest clouds
And gives my heart a song!

What Kind of King?

....

'The young men who had grown up with him replied, "Tell these
people who have said to you, 'Your father put a heavy yoke on us,
but make our yoke lighter' – tell them, 'My little finger is thicker
than my father's waist. My father laid on you a heavy yoke;
I will make it even heavier'"' (vv. 10, 11).

Rehoboam, son of Solomon, was poised to be the new king, so
Jeroboam hurried from Egypt to offer himself for the crown. There
could hardly have been two more different men. The older Israelites
longed for a less demanding life. They did not want another Solomon,
who made so many demands on them. That suited Jeroboam. But the
younger Israelites had appreciated Solomon's energy and creativity.
Rehoboam would be such a king. That was his style too.

And so the people of Israel faced a choice. The eventual result was
that the kingdom was divided. The twelve tribes had originally come
together at Shechem under Joshua, and had then been successively
ruled by three kings: Saul, David and Solomon. Now the twelve tribes
would divide into two kingdoms, north and south. Ten of the tribes –
those in the north – rejected Rehoboam's threat to impose an even
heavier yoke than Solomon and chose to be ruled by Jeroboam, the
rebel leader of Solomon's day. Only the tribes of Judah and Benjamin,
who occupied the southern lands of Judah, accepted Rehoboam as
their leader.

Perhaps the greatest significance of the division of the people of
Israel into two kingdoms is its recognition that Saul, David and
Solomon – despite their military and commercial successes – were
ultimately failures. All three kings were, in the end, found wanting.

The story of their nation following Solomon's death was to be, as
Bible scholar William Neil summarises it:

a sad and sordid one of disruption, intrigue, war and corruption . . .
Israel paid the price for playing at power politics, for aping the
common run of nations, for mistaking culture for covenant, for
becoming indistinguishable from any of the petty principalities
that staggered from one crisis to another in the ancient Mediter-
ranean world.[1]

Backslider Jeroboam

'After seeking advice, the king made two golden calves. He said to the people, "It is too much for you to go up to Jerusalem. Here are your gods, O Israel, who brought you up out of Egypt"' (v. 28).

After Jeroboam became king of the ten northern tribes of Israelites he was constantly worried that his people would decide to link up again with the two tribes in the south, ruled by Rehoboam. Jerusalem was in the south, and if Jeroboam's people carried on travelling there, to worship in the Temple, there was always the chance that they would transfer their allegiance to Rehoboam, who was of the house of David. He even spelt out his fear: 'They will kill me and return to King Rehoboam,' said Jeroboam (v. 27).

In the eyes of God's people, what Jeroboam proposed to do – manufacture idols – was the worst thing possible. Once before in their past they had abandoned the Almighty in favour of a golden calf; now here they were betraying their Lord once again. Disqualified people were made priests and the king set up altars in 'high places' to please foreign gods. It was a scandal, a national disaster waiting to happen. The division between Judah and Israel widened. Would the Israelites ever again be united? If Jeroboam had been acting for the good of his people that would at least have been something in his favour, but he merely wanted to save his own skin and his throne.

Down the ages there have been many leaders who manipulated their religion for their own good. Take England's Henry VIII; creating the Church of England and declaring himself head of it is a good example – or, rather, a bad one!

King Jeroboam knew well what happened to the first golden calf. Moses burned it, ground it into powder, mixed it with water and made the Israelites drink it! (See Exodus 32:20.) Did Jeroboam not see the danger of what he was doing? If he did, it didn't stop him. Sadly he was neither the first person, nor the last, to plough his own furrow regardless of the consequences.

The Mystery Man of God

....

'By the word of the LORD a man of God came from Judah to Bethel, as Jeroboam was standing by the altar to make an offering. He cried out against the altar by the word of the LORD: "O altar, altar!"' (vv. 1, 2).

This unnamed man of God was extremely courageous. To tell the king that one day a man from the house of David, called Josiah, would displace his descendents was a risky business, especially when he went on to say that the unworthy priests who officiated at Jeroboam's equally unworthy 'high places' would themselves be sacrificed. He failed to mention that they would have to wait 300 years for this to happen, but he did predict: '"The altar will be split apart and the ashes on it will be poured out"' (v. 3), and this time the prophecy was immediately fulfilled. It proved the integrity of the prophet and led Jeroboam to ask him to intercede on his behalf to the Lord.

As 'unnamed' people of God today, in the sense that few of us are famous for our faith, we should regard this anonymous prophet as a hero, and follow his brave example when we become aware of injustice and evil – whatever the consequences of our speaking out.

Sadly, Jeroboam, on hearing the prophet's words, was more angry than repentant. However, his call for the prophet to be arrested led to Jeroboam's own hand becoming shrivelled and useless. But at least, recognising the authenticity of the prophet, he had the humility to ask for healing, and received it.

But still Jeroboam did not mend his ways, not even after the incident recounted here of the deception and death of a man of God. Verse 33 tells us: 'Even after this, Jeroboam did not change his evil ways, but once more appointed priests for the high places from all sorts of people.' Jeroboam was a cunning man but was seemingly unable to learn from his mistakes, or those of other people.

We should take care to learn from Jeroboam what not to do.

....

To ponder:
'Courage, brother, do not stumble, though thy path be dark as night. There's a star to guide the humble; trust in God and do the right.'

Norman Macleod

God Insulted

'Jeroboam did not change his evil ways, but once more appointed priests for the high places from all sorts of people' (v. 33).

When the children of God turned away from him it was the consequence of their spiritual unhealthiness, which resulted in the re-establishment of unholy habits – perhaps most markedly prostitution in the context of sacred ceremonies.

King Jeroboam's disastrous fault was his lack of confidence in God. In his heart of hearts he simply did not believe God's resources were enough for his people. Jeroboam did not believe the Almighty was just that – almighty! He felt it necessary to turn to other gods for guidance, for wisdom, for protection. These other gods would be his 'back-up' if the traditional God of the Israelites needed reinforcements.

Specifically, Jeroboam betrayed God in the matter of 'high places'. These were not sanctified for offerings and sacrifices, but Jeroboam ruled that they were. Worse, the priests chosen by God were ignored and replaced by unqualified nobodies. God's prophets were not asked for direction, and when they bravely spoke up against this paganism they were punished, even slaughtered.

The temptation to take 'God supplements' is, sadly, a feature of twenty-first-century life. People worship material things, adore what is vulgar and obscene, and covet their neighbour's possessions. Although, strangely, many opinion polls record huge numbers of people declaring they believe in God, in many countries few give him any place in their lives. They never allow him to influence their attitudes, their priorities, their habits. Can an excluded God be called by that name? A shared throne is really no throne at all. It is an insult.

One of Jeroboam's great mistakes was in appointing priests 'from all sorts of people'. That was not healthy inclusivism, it was a rejection of God's stated plan. We should beware who we 'appoint' as our personal consultants, advisers, role models.

Jeroboam the Failure

'This is what the LORD, the God of Israel says: "I raised you up from among the people and made you a leader over my people Israel. I tore the kingdom away from the house of David and gave it to you, but you have not been like my servant David, who kept my commands and followed me with all his heart, doing only what was right in my eyes. You have done more evil than all who lived before you"' (vv. 7–9).

In this chapter we have a kind of end-of-school report for King Jeroboam. It was delivered to the king, via his wife, from the prophet Ahijah and it is far from glorious. The sins of the king are spelt out: you have been more evil than anybody. You have made for yourself other gods, idols made of metal. You have raised Asherah poles – worshipping images of the consort of the god Baal. You have raised altars for sacrifices to other gods. You have not kept my laws. You are nothing like King David.

The prophet's message continued, referring to the king's son: '"The boy will die. All Israel will mourn for him and bury him. He is the only one belonging to Jeroboam who will be buried, because he is the only one in the house of Jeroboam in whom the LORD, the God of Israel, has found anything good"' (vv. 12, 13).

What a verdict on Jeroboam! Verse 20 tells us: 'He reigned for twenty-two years' – but God found nothing good in him. What a failure! May our lives not cause God similar disappointment!

The chapter continues with a report on the life of King Rehoboam, who reigned in Jerusalem for seventeen years. He too was a less-than-great monarch, his people committing almost identical sins to those of Jeroboam's people.

Throughout the lives of Rehoboam and Jeroboam there was continued warfare. What a waste of time and wealth between related peoples! Once, both peoples had shared the same religion. They were all God's children. How sad the change! Happily, God's people today are at last displaying and enjoying a growing sense of unity, albeit a little gingerly!

Ponder . . . and praise!
All over the world God's Spirit is moving.

A Glimmer of Light!

*'Asa became king of Judah, and he reigned in Jerusalem forty-one
years . . . Asa did what was right in the eyes of the LORD,
as his father David had done' (vv. 9, 11).*

Chapters 15 and 16 are lamentable reports. So many of the kings
disappointed their God. Abijah, king of Judah – who 'committed all
the sins his father had done before him; his heart was not fully devoted
to the LORD his God' (v. 3) – mercifully reigned for only three years. It
was much the same with the kings before and after him. King Elah of
Israel, who reigned for just two years before being murdered by one of
his officials, Zimri, was busy getting drunk at the time of his death
(16:9, 10)!

Zimri declared himself king but failed in battle and set the royal
palace on fire around him. He died in the blaze. Perhaps it was suicide.
His sins and his unfaithfulness to God are recorded, as are those of
Omri, his successor. No wonder the people of God needed courageous
prophets. Or, better still, a Messiah.

There was one glimmer of light in those dark times. It was carried by
Asa, who reigned as king of Judah for forty-one years. He did what was
right in the eyes of the Lord. His reformations were dramatic. He
expelled the male prostitutes who operated at the shrines, and got rid
of the idols his forebears had made. He even deposed his grandmother,
the queen mother, for raising a worship pole for the goddess Asherah.
King Asa cut it down and burned it. He also brought back many of the
sacred furnishings of the Temple.

Sadly, his neighbour, King Ahab, mocked Asa's piety. Goodness and
faithfulness are not always appreciated. Nothing much changes, does
it?

Yield not to temptation, for yielding is sin;
Each victory will help you some other to win.
Fight manfully onward, dark passions subdue;
Look ever to Jesus, he will carry you through.
Horatio Richmond Palmer

God-expression

··

'When all things began, the Word already was. The Word dwelt with
God, and what God was, the Word was. The Word, then, was with
God at the beginning, and through him all things came to be . . .
So the Word became flesh; he came to dwell among us,
and we saw his glory' (vv. 1, 2, 14, NEB).

In the opening verses of his Gospel, John puts the incarnation of
Jesus into cosmic focus. But the fact remains that, through his
incarnation, Jesus brought God into human focus.

Beautifully Expressed!

When God expressed himself, the Word he spoke
Was clearly understood by ordinary folk.
They looked into his eyes, one single look sufficed.
Men read the mind of God, the face of Christ.
When Christ laid down his head upon a manger-bed,
His coming simply said: God is with you!
Kneeling upon the hay, we heard the Baby say:
Your God is here to stay; God is with you!
When Christ was crucified he hung his head and died;
His silenced body cried: God loves like this!
And still to us today, two thousand years away,
His suff'rings simply say: God loves like this!

The Prophet Needed!

'Ahab . . . not only considered it trivial to commit the sins of Jeroboam son of Nebat, but he also married Jezebel daughter of Ethbaal king of the Sidonians, and began to serve Baal and worship him. He . . . did more to provoke the LORD, the God of Israel, to anger than did all the kings of Israel before him' (vv. 30–33).

The devoted servants of God must have watched the behaviour of their kings with horror. They no doubt longed that someone would rescue them from Jezebel, who campaigned for the god called Baal. Soon the king himself became a follower of Baal and championed his cause. Where would it all end? Would the prophet Elijah be able to save the day? Three incidents give us the answer.

First, Elijah clashes with Ahab and warns the king there will soon be a shortage of water which will last as long as Elijah thinks it should. We can imagine Ahab asking, 'Who does Elijah think he is?' In those days, kings were used to making the decisions. But God looks after his servant, Elijah. He leads him to a safe place and provides ravens to feed him. Brave Elijah was not alone. No servant of God is abandoned when on duty.

In the second incident God shows his power through the story of a widow and a boy who share their tiny store of food with Elijah. By God's power, the jar of flour and jug of oil never run dry. We twenty-first-century people of God surely can take heart from this when we are in dire circumstances. God's provisions are limitless.

And the third incident? A mother's faith is tested when her son stops breathing. Elijah performs what we can only assume to be some kind of mouth-to-mouth resuscitation, but there was surely prayer in the equation, too. When God and one of his prophets combine their resources, anything can happen.

Let's observe and pray the prayer of the New Testament man whose son was cured by Jesus: ' "I do believe; help me overcome my unbelief" ' (Mark 9:24).

I do believe, I will believe, that Jesus died for me;
That on the cross he shed his blood, and now he sets me free.
William Cowper

Elijah – God's Man

'Elijah went before the people and said, "How long will you waver between two opinions? If the LORD is God, follow him; but if Baal is God, follow him"' (v. 21).

When Elijah went out to confront King Ahab, I wonder if the woman and her healed son were among the crowd of onlookers. And did the prophet remember what the widow at Zarephath said to him? If only the same could truthfully be said of all Christians: '"I know that you are a man of God and that the word of the LORD from your mouth is the truth"' (17:24).

Elijah must have trembled when his orders from God told him to go to Ahab and tell him that there would soon be rain after more than three years of drought. King Ahab probably blamed the prophet for the situation and could be looking for revenge!

On his journey Elijah met a good man called Obadiah. He was a devout believer in the Lord although he was in charge of the royal palace. Verse 4 of chapter 18 tells us: 'While Jezebel was killing off the LORD's prophets, Obadiah had taken a hundred prophets and hidden them in two caves, fifty in each, and had supplied them with food and water.' The assurance that at least one hundred prophets had survived must have warmed Elijah's heart.

Taking his life in his hands, at the request of Elijah, Obadiah told Ahab where to find his hated enemy. The exchange that followed is recorded in verses 16 to 39 and is well worth reading in full. It could be from a Hollywood screenplay! When the king calls Elijah a trouble-maker, the prophet answers: '"I have not made trouble for Israel . . . But you and your father's family have"' (v. 18).

Elijah refers to the disobedience and disloyalty of the king, then offers to face all the men of Israel and all the prophets of Baal and Asherah on Mount Carmel and take part in a challenge. What courage! What faith in God!

With the crowds present, Elijah comes straight to the point: '"How long will you waver between two opinions? If the LORD is God, follow him; but if Baal is God, follow him"' (v. 21). We hold our breath to see what will happen next.

The Lord is God!

••

' "You call upon the name of your god, and I will call on the name
of the LORD. The god who answers by fire – he is God."
Then all the people said: "What you say is good" ' (v. 24).

Elijah's confidence in his Lord was stunning. He must have been
conscious of the enormity of the risk he was taking. How clever he
was to give his opponents the first 'go'! Did the huge odds against him
sway the sympathy of the watching crowd in his direction? Certainly
the longer the prophets of Baal continued their ineffective attempts to
call down fire, the more the crowd's support for them evaporated.

Elijah's rebuilding of a once-ruined altar was a signal of his approaching victory. His use of twelve stones was a symbol not lost on anyone
watching. It suggested that the day would come when the divided
kingdom of Israel and Judah would be united again, all twelve tribes of
them.

The ecstatic pagan dancing and bodily mutilations of the priests had
no part in Elijah's plan. But no doubt his taunting of them did. They
were to be totally humiliated – hence Elijah's extravagant waste of
precious water to drench his altar. When the fire came there would be
no doubt of its miraculous, God-sent authenticity. Did Ahab begin to
tremble at this point?

The efforts of the prophets of Baal were futile. Then Elijah's turn
came. But it was not a time for boasting. He prayed: ' "O LORD, God of
Abraham, Isaac and Israel, let it be known today that you are God in
Israel and that I am your servant" ' (v. 36). The power and the glory
belonged to God. Elijah claimed and sought none for himself.

'Then the fire of the LORD fell' (v. 38). Note what was consumed: the
sacrifice, the wood, the stones, the soil, the water in the trench.
Nothing survived. And any doubt in the hearts of the observers was
consumed also. They fell on their faces and cried: ' "The LORD – he is
God! The LORD – he is God!" ' (v. 39).

It had taken a miracle to produce faith in those people. What does it
take to do the same in us?

The Aftermath

....

'Elijah commanded them, "Seize the prophets of Baal. Don't let anyone get away!" They seized them, and Elijah had them brought down to the Kishon Valley and slaughtered there' (v. 40).

It is difficult for us to understand the mind of Elijah. If he lived and behaved in this way in our day he would receive a psychiatric examination and then be imprisoned for life. He may not have spilled anyone's blood himself, but he gave the order. No doubt he sincerely believed he was doing God's will and that the Lord would be pleased that there were now 450 fewer prophets of Baal on the face of the earth. Elijah was a great man but, like everyone at that time, he had only a limited idea of the character of God.

We are different. We have seen God revealed in the life of Christ, who said: ' "Anyone who has seen me has seen the Father"' (John 14:9). How fortunate we are to have such a clear picture of God! But that bestows a huge responsibility on us to reflect something of his character in our lives.

How possible is that? In our own strength it's hard, but we don't have to rely on that – just as Elijah did not have to summon up fire on his own. God's Holy Spirit makes anything possible.

That thought led me to write the following, which surely expresses the ambition of every authentic Christian. It's certainly my testimony:

> To be like Jesus!
> This hope possesses me,
> In every thought and deed,
> This is my aim, my creed;
> To be like Jesus!
> This hope possesses me,
> His Spirit helping me,
> Like him I'll be.

Time of Depression?

'Elijah was afraid and ran for his life . . . he himself went a day's journey into the desert. He came to a broom tree, sat down under it and prayed that he might die. "I have had enough, LORD," he said. "Take my life; I am no better than my ancestors" ' (vv. 3, 4).

It's not hard to sympathise with Elijah. Most of us who have dedicated ourselves to an important task have known, at one time or another, the kind of depression which gripped the prophet. Typically on such occasions we think our work has not been appreciated and we have wasted our time. Sometimes self-pity or loneliness make the depression worse. Like Elijah, we've said: 'I have had enough, Lord.' We may not have wanted to die, but we've felt like packing up.

We don't know exactly who ministered to Elijah or how we should name the one who got him on his feet to enjoy fresh-baked bread. We call him or her an angel, one of God's agents, a God-send. (Incidentally, I've met more than one of these, and the place and time of their appearance has always been well chosen.) A couple of days' care from this servant of God gave the prophet strength to carry on for forty days and forty nights – a biblical way of saying 'a long time'.

Elijah's encounter with God is beautifully described. The wind, the earthquake and the fire came again as it had at Mount Carmel. But for this private, intimate conversation with his Lord, a gentle whisper was all that was needed.

What probably helped the prophet most was receiving new 'marching orders'. Elijah still had work to do for God. He was not discharged as no longer needed. And we can imagine the gentle whisper saying: 'By the way, please stop saying you are the only one left. I have still seven thousand followers in Israel who have never bowed down to Baal!' (v. 18, my paraphrase). God didn't quite say, 'Look on the bright side!' or 'Every cloud has a silver lining', but his reminder that things aren't always as bad as they seem is as worth bearing in mind today as then.

Elisha is Called

'Elisha then left his oxen and ran after Elijah. "Let me kiss my father and mother good-bye," he said, "and then I will come with you"' (v. 20).

The ceremony by which Elijah indicated that Elisha would inherit his prophet's role was simple. Elijah, finding Elisha in the middle of ploughing with twelve yoke of oxen, symbolically threw his cloak around him. Elisha responded by asking for permission to say goodbye to his family.

Elisha's subsequent slaughter of his oxen and burning of his ploughing tools indicated both that he was a wealthy man and that he had a change of priorities. Servants of God have felt compelled to indicate their allegiance in similar ways over the centuries – a sort of burning of boats to declare there will be no returning until the job is done.

Chapter 20:1–6 reveals the dangerous days in which the Israelites lived at that time. King Ahab of Israel was besieged in Samaria by King Ben-Hadad of Aram. The price of peace for Ahab was the giving-up of everything precious. Ben-Hadad's threat was simple: '"Your silver and gold are mine and the best of your wives and children are mine"' (v. 3). Ahab capitulated immediately and entirely, declaring cravenly: '"Just as you say, my lord the king. I and all I have are yours"' (v. 4).

How weak! Was there any hope for the kingdom of Israel?

Be strong in the grace of the Lord,
Be noble and upright and true.
Be valiant for God and the right,
Live daily your duty to do.
Be strong! Be strong!
And God will your courage renew.
Walter Henry Windybank

Scared? I Dare You!

••

'"Ask, and you will receive; seek, and you will find; knock,
and the door will be opened"' (v. 7, NEB).

Asking is dangerous. So is seeking. Knocking might open a door, on the other side of which could be either things I would die to discover or someone suggesting shattering changes to my way of living!

The Nerve to Knock

I do not pray, because I know you'll answer!
I dare not ask, for then I would receive!
My silence is not proof that I am faithless,
It only goes to show that I believe.
I do not seek, for fear that I might find you;
And finding you might well mean losing me!
And if I knocked, of course the door might open
And I would have to enter, don't you see?
Give me the nerve to knock, to seek, to ask, Lord;
To enter in, to find and to receive.
I don't doubt for a moment you will answer.
I tremble, Lord, because I do believe!

Unexpected Help

*'Meanwhile a prophet came to Ahab king of Israel and
announced, "This is what the LORD says: 'Do you see this vast army?
I will give it into your hand today, and then you will know that
I am the LORD'"' (v. 13).*

A hab had indicated that he would surrender to the massive army
united against his limited forces. But when he sought advice from
his counsellors and his people they urged him to resist King Ben-
Hadad, declaring: '"Don't listen to him or agree to his demands"' (v. 8).
This encouraged Ahab, who sent a defiant message to his enemy:
'"One who puts on his armour should not boast like one who takes it
off"' (v. 11). It's amazing how a little support from the people around
you can stiffen the will and make a timid man (or woman) brave.

Even more valuable support came to Ahab from the Almighty,
without even being specifically sought. An unnamed prophet of God
arrived with an announcement which was a promise of victory for
Israel's forces: '"I will give it into your hand today, and then you will
know that I am the LORD"' (v. 13).

We Christians often quote the words of Jesus: '"Ask, and it will be
given to you; seek and you will find; knock and the door will be opened
to you"' (Matthew 7:7). Sometimes we have nothing because we have
asked for nothing. But the benevolence of God is such that often we
receive before we ask. Many of us can recall such occasions. They are
often undeserved blessings.

Ask the Saviour to help you,
Comfort, strengthen and keep you;
He is willing to aid you,
He will carry you through.
                    Horatio Richmond Palmer

Dirty Tricks

Jezebel his wife said, "Is this how you act as king over Israel?
Get up and eat! Cheer up. I'll get you the vineyard of
Naboth the Jezreelite"' (v. 7).

The good man Naboth was not just being difficult with his king when he refused to sell his vineyard to the monarch. King Ahab knew very well that the land owned by Naboth's family was almost a sacred area, which they regarded as held by them as if on a lease from the Almighty. For Ahab to even ask to buy it was something of an insult. Other nations – the Canaanites, for example – allowed their kings special liberties, but in Israel even royalty had limitations on their privileges, and Ahab was overstepping the mark here.

The incident drew out the ugly side of King Ahab, who sulked when he could not get his own way and even refused to eat. Even worse, he expected his wife to do his dirty work for him. Did he blush, I wonder, when she responded by telling him: '"Get up and eat! . . . I'll get you the vineyard"' (v. 7)?

Did Ahab realise Jezebel would use dirty tricks to get what he wanted, involving a couple of crooks whose lies condemned innocent Naboth to death by stoning for the offence of cursing both God and the king? Whatever, Ahab stopped sulking once he was free to take possession of the vineyard he so much wanted. Was this really the same man who had been anointed with sacred oil in God's name? Should our God – a God of honesty, justice, compassion and purity – have to deal with such scoundrels?

But before we rush to judgment – however deservedly – we should pause and remember our own shortcomings. Even the best of us is far from perfect in the light of the holiness we so desperately aim for in our better moments.

To ponder:
'There is no single definition of holiness . . . but there is one I am particularly fond of: being holy means getting up immediately every time you fall, with humility and joy. It doesn't mean never falling into sin. It means being able to say: "yes, Lord, I have fallen a thousand times. But thanks to you I have got up again a thousand and one times."'

Helder Camara

Repentance and Forgiveness

*'"Go down to meet Ahab king of Israel, who rules in Samaria.
He is now in Naboth's vineyard, where he has gone to take possession
of it. Say to him, 'This is what the LORD says: Have you not
murdered a man and seized his property?'"' (vv. 18, 19).*

A prophet's lot is neither easy nor pleasant. To accuse anyone – let alone a king – of being a murderer and a thief requires much courage and a great deal of confidence in the One who gives you that task. Elijah did as he was commanded and went even further. He told the king what the punishment from God would be. Elijah could not have been more explicit: '"In the place where dogs licked up Naboth's blood, dogs will lick up your blood – yes, yours!"' (v. 19).

Ahab recognised that the game was up. '"So you have found me, my enemy!"' he told Elijah, who responded: '"I have found you because you have sold yourself to do evil in the eyes of the LORD"' (v. 20). The consequence would be that Ahab's family would be wiped out, including Jezebel, who would be eaten by dogs. Such a verdict would not have surprised the people of Israel. Moses gave them the principle of 'an eye for an eye' and there was little room for mercy in those days.

However, mercy there would be, even for Ahab, as a result of his repentance. When Ahab saw what lay ahead for him he expressed his deep regrets for his sins, especially his idol worship. In the light of this, God relented: '"Have you noticed how Ahab has humbled himself before me? Because he has humbled himself, I will not bring this disaster in his day"' (v. 29). And if Ahab's sons straightened things out perhaps there would be mercy for them also. Time would tell!

To ponder:
'The humble man receives praise the way a clean window takes the light of the sun. The truer and more intense the light is, the less you see of the glass.'

Thomas Merton

Unreliable Prophets

> '"Is there not a prophet of the LORD here whom we can inquire of?"
> The king of Israel answered Jehoshaphat, "There is still one man
> through whom we can inquire of the LORD, but I hate him because he
> never prophesies anything good about me, but always bad. He is
> Micaiah"' (vv 7, 8).

The imperfections of unauthentic prophecy are well illustrated here. Fortune tellers have a tendency to say what the customer wants to hear, and some bogus prophets do the same. 'Cross my palm with silver,' says the fortune teller and the customer gets his or her worthless reward.

True prophets of God must be honest, trustworthy and single-minded. They must listen carefully to the Lord and pass on God's message truthfully – even when they receive a beating, or worse, for their pains. King Ahab hated the prophet Micaiah because Micaiah did just this, even though he knew Ahab preferred soft lies to hard truth.

The king of Israel wanted to go to war accompanied by the king of Judah, and more than four hundred prophets told him he would be victorious. But Micaiah knew otherwise. He had received a vision from God (vv. 19, 20) and told the king the enterprise would be a disaster. Everyone should go home in peace.

King Ahab would have none of it. '"Didn't I tell you that he never prophesies anything good about me, but only bad?"' he declared (v. 18), and ordered that Micaiah should be imprisoned on bread and water until he, Ahab, returned (v. 27). But Micaiah had the last word: '"If you ever return safely, the LORD has not spoken through me"' (v. 28).

Few of us may count ourselves prophets, but the Lord needs all his followers to be as faithful to the truth as Micaiah was. His reputation, as well as ours, depends upon it.

To ponder:
**'God is faithful, and if we serve him faithfully, he will provide
for our needs.'**

St Richard of Chichester

If Only . . .

'Someone drew his bow at random and hit the king of Israel between the sections of his armour. The king told his chariot driver, "Wheel around and get me out of the fighting. I've been wounded"' (v. 34).

Although Ahab decided to press on with the war against the king of Aram, Micaiah's warning about the outcome scared him, and he tried his best to protect himself. One of his tactics was to disguise himself. Perhaps he knew the king of Aram had told his thirty-two chariot commanders, '"Do not fight with anyone, small or great, except the king of Israel"' (v. 31). As it happened, Ahab was wounded by a stray arrow that had not been aimed specifically at him. No bowman could claim the credit for the royal wounds.

In those far-distant days, when the leader fell, his army collapsed. This occasion was no exception. The king was propped up in his chariot and his blood ran onto the floor, fulfilling Elijah's prophesy. Ahab did not survive the day. 'As the sun was setting a cry spread through the army: "Every man to his town; everyone to his land!"' (v. 36).

If only Ahab had listened to Micaiah! If only everyone had gone home in peace, as the prophet recommended! Sadly, it's not unusual for a prophet to be ignored. Let's remember that God is interested in every aspect of our lives, and seeks to guide us in a variety of ways. And let's be on the lookout for his prophets, however their messages are delivered.

In this connection, consider these words of William Temple: 'The prophet is primarily the man not to whom God has communicated certain thoughts but whose mind is illuminated by the divine Spirit to interpret aright the divine acts.'

A *prayer*:

> Master, speak: and make me ready,
> When thy voice is truly heard,
> With obedience glad and steady
> Still to follow every word.
> I am listening, Lord, for thee;
> Master, speak: O speak to me!
> *Frances Ridley Havergal*

They Might Have Done Better?

'In everything he [Jehoshaphat, king of Judah] walked in the ways of his father Asa and did not stray from them; he did what was right in the eyes of the LORD. The high places, however, were not removed, and the people continued to offer sacrifices and burn incense there' (v. 43).

The monarchs whose stories are told in the first book of Kings were a very mixed bag. They were clearly subject to the temptations which beset all human beings, and frequently gave in to them. But some ruled wisely and well, at least some of the time.

Jehoshaphat, king of Judah, had many good traits. He walked in the ways of his godly father Asa and 'did what was right in the eyes of the LORD' (v. 43). He rid the land of male religious prostitutes – something even his father had not achieved – and his reign was mostly a time of peace. But he did not wipe out pagan worship sites known as 'high places'. Did he run out of time? But he was king for twenty-five years – long enough, surely? Perhaps his priorities could have been better. That could be said of many of us.

The last king recorded in this book is Ahaziah of Israel. Sadly, there was not a good word that could be said of him. It seems he did everything wrong and provoked God to anger.

As for Jezebel's ultimate fate, to know that we must wait until we turn the pages of the second book of Kings. If you cannot wait that long, the answer is in 2 Kings 9. Here's a clue: the prophecy was not wrong.

The history recorded in the Old Testament is largely the stories of prophets and kings. We can learn from both. But the ordinary men and women of Israel and surrounding lands had their part to play. We can learn from them too. They were wise when they listened to the prophets, and even wiser when they obeyed the word of the Lord. If only their kings – and queens – had done more of that!

To ponder:
'Every duty, even the least duty, involves the whole principle of obedience. And little duties make the will dutiful that is supple and prompt to obey. Little obediences lead into great.'

Henry E. Manning

Christmas is Coming!

●●

'"I have come that men may have life, and may have it in all its
fullness"' (John 10:10, NEB).

My experience is that *happiness* is temporary. It lasts a while and we should be grateful for it. *Joy* has a finer quality and something permanent about it. Happiness can evaporate rapidly. Joy has solid foundations and is less dependent upon circumstances. Jesus explained that he came into the world to bring us life – the real thing. Joy is a product of that life.

Joy comes with Jesus

Joy fills the heart of ev'ry friend of Jesus.
Joy fills the heart where Jesus has his throne.
Joy without him is but a fleeting phantom.
Joy that endures is his and his alone.
Proclaim the message, fling it to the skies:
Joy comes with Jesus. Joy which never dies!
Sad is the heart that never knew the Saviour.
Sick is the soul that never felt his touch.
God loved his world and sent his Son to save it.
God loves his world, the cross reveals how much.
How will men know unless we make it plain?
Joy comes with Jesus. There's no other name!
Pointless is life without his precious presence.
Empty the life where Jesus is not King.
Without the Christ, there is no rhyme or reason.
Without the Christ, no sense in anything.
Success is tasteless. Wealth is just a toy.
Joy comes with Jesus. Jesus is our joy!

How Far is it to Bethlehem?

Introduction

This Advent series has been prepared by Commissioner Robert Street who, since becoming a Salvation Army officer in 1969 with his wife, Janet, has served in a rich variety of appointments – as a corps officer in England, as editor of the UK War Cry for ten years and then as editor-in-chief, before taking on the roles of divisional commander in Anglia and then Principal of William Booth College, London. Prior to coming to his present assignment as International Secretary to the Chief of the Staff, International Headquarters, he served in Sydney as Chief Secretary of the Australia Eastern Territory.

Whatever his appointment, he has used writing as a vital tool in his ministry. Among his recent publications are Servant Leadership and Holiness Unwrapped, both of which have been translated into a number of languages. Robert writes:

'How far is it to Bethlehem?' is the first line and title of a Christmas poem written by Frances Chesterton, wife of renowned poet G. K. Chesterton. In these Advent readings, I trace the path to Bethlehem of some of the main characters in the Bible narratives, examining their attitudes, what the journey required of them, and what might have been the cost involved.

As we look at the biblical accounts we too are encouraged to make our own pilgrimage to the humble cave in Bethlehem where Jesus Christ, the Saviour of the world, was born. We may also discover that the answer to the question 'how far?' very much depends on us.

For the Sunday readings in December, John Gowans continues to provide a prayer-poem with his selected Bible passage.

Welcome to Bethlehem

....

'"But you, Bethlehem Ephrathah, though you are small among the clans of Judah, out of you will come for me one who will be ruler over Israel, whose origins are from of old, from ancient times"' (v. 2).

My first visit to Bethlehem was in the 1980s. It didn't take long for my Christmas-card image to be shattered. I hadn't anticipated being greeted by angels, shepherds and wise men – or even by a harassed innkeeper – but the sheer poverty of the place immediately brought me face to face with stark reality. Shops were boarded up. Traders had gone out of business or been taken over by their wealthy, more powerful competitors, and the graffiti scrawled across crumbling walls added insult to injury.

Then I noticed the soldiers. They were armed and edgy. They were expecting trouble and disturbances. They were not wanted. They were seen as the enemy, occupying Palestinian land. Poorly dressed children, who had learnt how to antagonise the soldiers, were also skilled in selling memorabilia and religious trinkets to the tourists. The spirit of Christmas seemed a million miles away.

My journey to Bethlehem hadn't involved a million miles – just two thousand – but the journey had been more than worthwhile. I realised afresh that the world into which the Son of God was born had been a world of poverty, conflict, danger and risk. There had also been an occupying power – from Rome.

Jesus didn't arrive as a tourist. Nor did he visit as a monarch expecting adulation and respect. He came exposed to the worst humankind could (and would) throw at him. As we make our journey to Bethlehem together, we also must embrace the reality of the world in which we live and are invited to serve – if we truly want to discover the depth, strength and liberating power of all that Christ came to bring.

....

A prayer:
Lord, save me from being a spiritual tourist.

War and Peace

••

'And he will be their peace' (v. 5).

Bethlehem has a long, influential history. It existed as a village as early as the time of Jacob. Rachel was buried there (Genesis 35:19) and her tomb is still acknowledged. It is also, more significantly, noted as the birthplace of King David – who is remembered, among other things, as a great warrior.

Bethlehem has a history of violence. Its violent history is seen both before and after the arrival of Jesus. During the reign of David his home town fell into the hands of the Philistines (2 Samuel 23:14). Since the birth of Christ it has been the scene of many skirmishes and battles. The Persian invasion of AD 614 and the rule of al-Hakim in the eleventh century are both conflicts which centred on religious power and domination. Ironically, battles have been waged and people slaughtered in Bethlehem to defend or attack the Christian and other faiths.

Yet Micah tells us: 'And he will be their peace' (v. 5). Knowing he would be misunderstood, misrepresented and the subject of strife through the ages, Jesus still came – bringing peace. It's a long way to travel if your journey of reconciliation is going to be wasted, but Jesus saw beyond our debasing of what is good. Nations will be at war until the end of time, but Jesus knew the eternal worth of what he was bringing.

Jesus never forced himself on people during his days on earth. It would have been entirely out of character. God doesn't work like that. Had he decided that subduing his creatures by force was appropriate, he wouldn't have come as a baby. Forced relationships, forced compliance, forced love do not work.

As we travel to Bethlehem we are urged by Jesus to see the wisdom of his costly approach. We are invited to embrace his gentle yet uncompromising attitude to others (Matthew 11:28), and at times, like him, to suffer its pain. It is the only way to true relationship with him and with others – and to peace of heart.

••

To do:
'Let the peace of Christ rule in your hearts.'

(Colossians 3:15)

Just Kneel

··

'"Does not the Scripture say that the Christ will come from David's family and from Bethlehem, the town where David lived?"' (v. 42).

There have always been arguments about the actual birthplace of Jesus. Proving the time and place two thousand years on is simply not possible, but it's interesting to see that people of Jesus' day also managed to argue about where he came from. John's Gospel shows how his credentials as 'the Christ' were doubted because he was known to be from Nazareth in Galilee. Nazareth was not held in high regard (John 1:46).

The early Christian practice of building churches on holy sites has encouraged belief that the location of the Nativity Church in Bethlehem is authentic. The first known church constructed there goes back to the fourth century when Helena, mother of Roman Emperor Constantine, ensured that the site was recognised. It was rebuilt by Justinian in the 530s and is thought to have survived the Persian invasion of 614 because of depictions of the Magi on its walls. Friendly local relationships between Muslims and Christians are given as the reason for its survival in the eleventh century.

On my first visit to the church I was shown the cave-like room under the building where tradition says Jesus came into the world. Our guide was specific. Pointing to two different parts of the room, she said, 'This is where Jesus was born and this is where they laid him.' Not surprisingly, there were those among the group who viewed such confident information with suspicion.

On a later visit I was in a queue of people waiting, sometimes impatiently, for their turn to enter the cave. There was some pushing and shoving which seemed misplaced. Then I noticed a young couple kneeling on the corner of the stairs which led into the room. They were oblivious to the arguments going on around them. They were kneeling in prayer. They were lost in worship. They had remembered the purpose of their journey.

There is still some pushing and shoving in the Church today – jostling for position – as well as unedifying arguments over insignificant things. Let's remember the purpose of our pilgrimage – and just kneel.

It Depends from where You Start

'The fool says in his heart, "There is no God" ' (v. 1).

Just how far it is to Bethlehem geographically depends on the starting point of our journey. Those starting from Jerusalem have less than ten kilometres to travel. Those starting from Australia, Chile or Alaska have a few thousand.

The same principle applies spiritually. There are those who, in a sense, are already halfway to Bethlehem. They have been nurtured in the Christian faith from childhood and have responded to the invitation to seek relationship with Jesus Christ. Others have been taught to be suspicious. Their parents, or other influential people in their lives, have cautioned them against religion. They have warned them off, viewing worship as deluded and prayer as something strange. There are variations on these examples, but they remind us that we each start our journey from a different place.

Perhaps we should trace back and analyse why we think and believe as we do. Have we advanced from the teaching or reasoning we received as impressionable children? Have we broadened our thinking? Are we open to what God in Christ may have to say to us today – or are we still trapped in the influence of the past?

The psalmist tells us the fool has decided there is no God. Some people may be 'fools' simply because they were taught to disbelieve, or because they have never investigated matters for themselves – they haven't begun the journey to Bethlehem and see no reason for it.

There are other reasons for finding ourselves a long way away from worshipping Jesus. Among them is fear of what knowing him might mean for us personally. We understand enough to assess there are implications.

For some people there are hurts to overcome – including hurts caused by Christians. There are disappointments, regrets and misunderstandings. There is also disillusionment, bitterness and pride. All these act as barriers and put us at a distance from God. Yet these are the very things he invites us to bring to him – for healing.

Helping Others Find the Way

....

'". . . to make ready a people prepared for the LORD"' (v. 17).

Whenever angels are mentioned in the birth narrative their appearance always startles. In today's reading, Zechariah is 'startled' and 'gripped with fear' (v. 12). When Mary is visited by Gabriel she is recorded as being 'greatly troubled' (Luke 1:29). In Luke 2 the shepherds reacted with terror (v. 9). Although the appearance of angels would have been surprising (to say the least), the initial reaction of those visited wasn't.

On every occasion the angel concerned took immediate steps to calm troubled souls. 'Do not be afraid' was the automatic response. It was necessary to help those being startled to regain a fit state to take in the message.

In Zechariah's case the message was that his wife was to have the baby that long ago they had accepted would never come. But there were instructions too. Their son's purpose on earth was clearly stated. First, Zechariah was told, '"He will be a joy and delight to you"' (v. 14). This was good news indeed – the human touch! Then the message continued: '"and many will rejoice because of his birth, for he will be great in the sight of the Lord . . . and he will be filled with the Holy Spirit even from birth"' (vv. 14–16).

This is more than enough to make any prospective father beam with pride, but there's more: '"Many of the people of Israel will he bring back to the Lord their God. And he will go on before the Lord . . . to make ready a people prepared for the Lord"' (vv. 16, 17). His task was to prepare the way for people to understand, meet and respond to Jesus.

In the same way that the angels prepared the way for an understanding of the birth and place of Jesus, so John (to become known as the Baptiser) was also to prepare the way among his people, to help them to be ready for the adult Christ who would live among them.

We may or may not make an actual journey to Bethlehem, but we each can help others find their way to the Saviour.

....

To ponder:
Who am I currently helping to find Jesus?

God at Work

'"Greetings, you who are highly favoured! The Lord is with you"'
(v. 28).

Mary isn't the only person recorded in Scripture as having been told 'the Lord is with you'. Gideon is among those greeted with the same words (Judges 6:12). Their appointed tasks were vastly different – and so were their responses. Gideon's reaction was to ask why the world was in such a mess if God was truly with him (6:13). Mary wanted to know what God might want of her (Luke 1:29).

Not much has changed in human responses. Today there are mixed reactions to the news that God loves us unreservedly. Some think it's too good to be true. They decide that there must be 'a catch' some-where, and they wonder why God seems absent at crucial times. Why doesn't he intervene when we need him most?

But to ask for God's intervention is to assume he is not acting already. Perhaps it also makes a further assumption that we know best and care more, or that he needs us to prompt him into action. The birth narrative reminds us that God is already at work and it is we who need to learn how to co-operate with him.

Luke tells us that God sent the angel Gabriel. It was divine initiative. So was the message. '*You will* be with child . . . *you are* to give him the name Jesus . . . *He will* be great . . . the *Lord God* will give him the throne of his father David . . . and *he will* reign over the house of Jacob for ever; *his kingdom will* never end.'

This is not the message of a God who has forgotten the needs of his creation. These are the words of a God at work, caring supremely.

> Christ stepped from the safety of heaven
> To walk with the human race,
> He left the warmth of his Father's home
> To give a cold world his embrace.
> The path that he trod brought him suffering,
> Ended with death on a tree;
> But the bridge that he built lasts for ever
> And spans eternity.
>
> R. S.

Christmas Gifts

....

'Out of his full store we have all received grace upon grace'
(v. 16, NEB).

Each of us has received at least three magnificent gifts! First, 'the right to become children of God' (v. 12); next, 'we have all received grace upon grace' (v. 16, *NEB*) – that means a gift beyond beauty and beyond measure and beyond deserving; then, in Jesus, God has given us a picture of himself: 'he has made him known' (v. 18, *NEB*). Only Jesus could do that.

The Gift of Himself

'What are you doing here?' I said,
When I found Christ had made his bed
In my cow-dung-floored cattle shed.
'Where better could I be?' he smiled,
'Than wrapped up in a little child?
Divinity will lay his head
In anybody's manger bed!
I've made myself a little place
Here with the hurting human race.
A Saviour's work is hard I fear,
But that's what I am doing here!
I'd love to be your Saviour, too,
And that's why I've moved in with you!'
In timber trough new truth I find.
Can God incarnate be so kind?
He's doing this with me in mind!

The Path of Obedience

....

' "I am the Lord's servant," Mary answered. "May it be
to me as you have said" ' (v. 38).

This was the perfect response. Chosen by God to fulfil his will in a unique and never-to-be repeated way, Mary surrendered herself to whatever the Lord required. Her journey to Bethlehem was by the path of obedience. We shouldn't be surprised to read that Mary had already found favour with God. He knew her servant heart.

The Bible records varied responses from men and women chosen by God for a particular task. Moses made his excuses and argued – eventually accepting his divine appointment (Exodus 3 and 4). Jonah ran off and tried to escape from his preaching assignment in Nineveh (Jonah 1:3). The 'rich young ruler' found Jesus' conditions too hard to embrace – and walked away (Matthew 19:22). Peter and Andrew made an immediate positive response (Mark 1:18).

Without obedience Mary would have never realised her destiny. She would never have known the depth of experience involved in caring for God's 'one and only' Son (John 3:16) – of having the privilege of knowing and supporting the world's Saviour in a way no other person ever could. Of course, to have excused herself would also have meant avoiding the pain of watching him go to the cross and his death.

And yet, because she was obedient, she was privileged to play a unique role in the redemption of the world. Put simply, the baby delivered of her was to become our world's deliverer – and therefore hers too.

When Jesus was at a wedding in Cana, Mary told some servants, ' "Do whatever he tells you" ' (John 2:5). She was recommending to others what she had been doing for years – even before the birth of her son. The lesson of Mary's gracious and unequivocal obedience is worth learning.

....

To ponder:
What excuses do I make for my lack of obedience?

Nothing is Impossible with God

••

*'"Blessed is she who has believed that what the Lord has
said to her will be accomplished!"' (v. 45).*

At the same time as hearing about her own impending motherhood,
Mary was told of Elizabeth's pregnancy (v. 36), so she travelled the
short distance to her relative's home to talk things over. It would have
been an exciting meeting, neither woman hardly daring to believe
what was happening. Yet believe is exactly what they both did.

Elizabeth's husband, Zechariah, had been struck dumb through his
unbelief (v. 20). Elizabeth had an altogether different approach. Her
words to Mary are full of faith. She concludes them by drawing attention to Mary's confidence in what God had promised: '"Blessed is she
who has believed that what the Lord has said to her will be accomplished!"' (v. 45). Our lives would benefit immeasurably from such
faith.

We share the promises of Scripture. They tell us that the Lord has
redeemed us, that we will never be outside his eternal caring presence
and that 'no eye has seen, no ear has heard, no mind conceived what
God has prepared for those who love him' (1 Corinthians 2:9). If only
we lived believing it!

Luke's narrative includes the promise that '"nothing is impossible
with God"' (1:37). These words are spoken by Gabriel in the context of
Elizabeth becoming pregnant *within the purposes of God.* Sometimes we
fall into the trap of imagining that 'anything is possible' without
remembering that every prayer must first be surrendered to the
purposes of God. To forget leads to false and unrealistic expectations
and to a misunderstanding of our relationship with him.

Our prayers will be less disappointing and our faith truly
strengthened when we learn, like Mary, to pray 'your will be done' –
and leave the rest with him.

••

To ponder:
**To what extent are my prayers self-centred or centred in the
purposes of God?**

Joy from Obedience

* *

'"My soul glorifies the Lord and my spirit rejoices in God my Saviour"' (vv. 46, 47).

Mary's prayer, known as the Magnificat, is as full an expression of gratitude to God as we are ever likely to encounter. Thanksgiving resounds in every line. Her joy is unbounded. Her praise unconfined. Mary is at peace within herself and in harmony with God – and it shows.

Such joy seems all too rare – tantalisingly illusive. Even in what may promise to be our highest moments, there can be an indefinable something that gets in the way of knowing the 'fulness of joy' mentioned in Psalm 16:11 (*KJV*). But not for Mary. What is her secret? It is her obedience – her complete surrender to the will of God. Her obedience is not a chore, not a burden. It is the means by which she finds true joy.

In *A God Who Acts*, Harry Blamires says, 'The only true joy is obedience to God.'[2] Anything less brings barriers, reservations and guilt. Even our praise of God won't ring true unless it is accompanied by obedience. Blamires continues: 'Since every gift we receive from God comes with a command attached to it, the sum of our argument is this: that gratitude means obedience.'

If we are truly grateful it will be shown in our obedience. The equation is clear: gratitude equals obedience equals joy.

* *

> Love Divine, all loves excelling,
> Joy of Heaven, to earth come down,
> Fix in us thy humble dwelling,
> All thy faithful mercies crown.
> Jesus, thou art all compassion,
> Pure, unbounded love thou art;
> Visit us with thy salvation,
> Enter every longing heart.
>
> *Charles Wesley*

The Path of Trust

'He had in mind to divorce her quietly' (v. 19).

It's hardly surprising that Joseph had in mind to set aside the marriage contract when he discovered Mary was pregnant. That he was prepared to do so quietly was an indication of his desire to protect her from any more public disgrace than necessary.

He must have been in turmoil. He had trusted Mary implicitly, sensing she was a godly and virtuous woman. Her unexpected pregnancy didn't make sense. He deserved an explanation and Matthew tells us he got one. In a dream an angel told him: ' "Joseph son of David, do not be afraid to take Mary home as your wife, because what is conceived in her is from the Holy Spirit" ' (v. 20).

Subsequent events show that Joseph followed instructions – and trusted that God was in control. If Mary trod the path of obedience to Bethlehem, Joseph's path was one of trust. He could have interpreted events in any number of ways and have reacted in rebellion at his manhood being relegated to a caretaker role. But in spite of his feelings, he 'hung in there' and trusted. He obeyed too.

The roles we are each asked to undertake by God in the fulfilling of his purposes are not always plain. Sometimes they make sense to us; they are clearly understood and seem in harmony with what we know – and possibly with what pleases us. At other times, what we are called upon to do for God is in conflict with either our mind or our heart – perhaps both. At such times we need the trust of Joseph until the picture becomes clearer. It may be, of course, that we carefully arrange our lives so as to avoid any real need for deep trust in God.

Whatever the case, even if the picture doesn't become clear in this life, God can be trusted to know what he is doing.

To ponder:
Which is the harder – trusting or obeying?

The Path of Response

'"Let's go to Bethlehem and see this thing that has happened,
which the Lord has told us about"' (v. 15).

The shepherds didn't have as far to travel as Mary and Joseph. They were already in Bethlehem – on the outskirts, in the fields with their sheep. Nor did they have to do a great deal of research or soul-searching. They were given the news with startling clarity. The angel told them what was happening and where the event had taken place – even down to the information that the baby was 'wrapped in cloths and lying in a manger' (v. 12).

Luke's narrative paints a picture of some ordinary people receiving extraordinary news and immediately responding. The words 'so they hurried off' indicate excitement, probably mixed with a huge dose of curiosity – a Saviour, in a manger, wrapped in cloths?

For many today the journey to Bethlehem – the one that ends in us kneeling in worship of God's Son – isn't that simple. We live in an analytical age of suspicion, cynicism and hesitancy about matters of faith. The clear messages of Scripture are more available than ever, and in many forms and translations, but immediate wholehearted response is sometimes hard to find. Responding to a simple message is somehow too difficult.

By today's standards the shepherds might be thought naïve, but they had the sense to go and see for themselves – and it was in the seeing that they found the news to be true. Having made the discovery they then 'spread the word' (v. 17). They just couldn't keep it to themselves.

People who discover Jesus today still behave in much the same way as the shepherds. The joy of what they have found cannot be contained What a pity if our pride or suspicion means we never get that far!

A prayer:
Lord, give me an openness to you and your message, and a readiness to respond.

Following the Light

'"We saw his star in the east and have come to worship him"' (v. 2).

There are different theories about the Magi – where they came from, who they represented, what kind of 'wise men' they were, and how long it was before they arrived. Nobody actually knows. They are generally accepted as having been astrologers of some kind, who arrived two years after the birth of Jesus. But although the word 'magic' is derived from the same Greek root as *magi*, there is no indication to suggest that these eastern visitors practised sorcery or claimed magical powers. In his commentary Matthew Henry puts it like this: 'Whatever sort of wise men they were before . . . they began to be wise men indeed when they set themselves to enquire after Christ.'

A common ancient belief was that a new star appeared at the time of a ruler's birth, and this seems to have prompted the search (v. 2). Their journey – made with the intention of worshipping the new king – has ever since been representative of people who 'follow the light'.

Jesus often spoke of light. In fact he claimed to be the light of the world (John 8:12). He also promised that those who seek God would find him (Matthew 7:7). Wherever they were in their ongoing quest for God, the Magi followed the light they had been given with enthusiasm and energy. Intelligent, cultured and respected, they were not too proud to follow the light – and seek.

The success of their journey can encourage us to follow their example.

> As with gladness men of old
> Did the guiding star behold,
> As with joy they hailed its light,
> Leading onward, beaming bright,
> So, most gracious Lord, may we
> Ever more be led to thee.
> *William Chatterton Dix*

Christmas Card

∙∙

'God was in Christ reconciling the world to himself, no longer holding men's misdeeds against them, and . . . he has entrusted us with the message of reconciliation' (v. 19, NEB).

We have a message that matches the hour!

My Card?

The Baby cries again this year, as ev'ry year.
And I must think of God in Christ again, I fear,
And comprehend, that's if I can,
How God could wrap himself in man!
If God should want to speak to man, say something good,
The words he chose would have to be well understood.
One single lovely Word he said,
And laid it in a manger bed.
If I have glimpsed the truth at all, I've understood
That God once dressed himself, with man, in flesh and blood,
Crossed the gulf of time and space
And came to join the human race!
My finite mind, my fumbling thoughts, still find it hard
To grasp the message printed on my Christmas card:
That God's superb redemption plan
In Bethl'em's borrowed barn began!
I can't explain the ageless truth of love expressed,
I only know in Jesus all the world is blessed.
And when I look into his face
I'm glad God joined the human race!

So Near but so Far

'He gave orders to kill all the boys in Bethlehem and its vicinity who were two years old and under, in accordance with the time he had learned from the Magi' (v. 16).

In spite of his long reign, King Herod had always felt insecure. Plagued by fears of plots and conspiracies against him, he ordered the deaths of family members and others he saw as rivals to his throne. His instruction to kill all the boys in and around Bethlehem was in keeping with how he had ruled throughout. Herod the Great displayed anything but greatness.

If the Magi surprised him by inquiring where the king was to be born (v. 2), his own advisers sent him into a panic by telling him that Scripture pointed to 'a ruler' for Israel coming from Bethlehem (v. 6) – less than ten kilometres down the road. Evidently, the wise men were indeed wise enough to avoid letting Herod know where Jesus was (v. 12), but this merely enraged him and the massacre was ordered.

Mary and Joseph escaped to Egypt with Jesus, but the horror of what happened in and around Bethlehem leaves us asking how anyone could order – 'or carry out – such carnage. Some comfort might be found if we could dismiss this kind of event as a quirk of history – a 'one off' – but such massacres still occur in our twenty-first-century world.

As we raise our hands in horror at human inhumanity, it is worth reminding ourselves that less dramatic cruelties are occurring every day in 'respectable' homes and communities. Some children – unloved, abused or regularly bullied – have their life drained out of them before they have begun to live.

There is also a subtle tendency in some of us to humiliate – even 'destroy' – others in a vain hope to make ourselves look big. Significantly, Jesus did the reverse. He made himself of 'no reputation' but now has the 'name which is above every name' (Philippians 2:7, 9, *KJV*).

Herod's behaviour is a warning. He was so near to Bethlehem, yet so far from *the* kingdom.

The Longest Journey

*'In the beginning was the Word, and the Word was with God,
and the Word was God' (v. 1).*

John gives no birth narratives. Instead, he puts Christ's coming to earth in its eternal perspective: 'In the beginning was the Word' (v. 1). The Word of God (revealed eventually in verse 29 as Jesus) has existed from the beginning – before all time. He was active in all creation. The life within him is the light of men. By making these statements, John sets Jesus apart from mere people, even though he tells us he is truly 'made flesh' and became a human being (v. 14).

There are those who suggest that John, the last to write his Gospel, gave this perspective because the divinity of Jesus was being challenged by some Christians. The other Gospels had given strong records of his activity and teaching. This Gospel was now designed to emphasise the depth of spiritual meaning behind it all.

As we try to think of Jesus' coming to earth in terms of a journey we acknowledge the impossibility of fully grasping its implications. It involves distance and dimensions, time and eternity, grace and giving. Charles Wesley suggests there was also a shedding of privilege and honour:

> He left his Father's throne above,
> So free, so infinite his grace,
> Emptied himself of all but love
> *And bled for Adam's helpless race . . .*

The apostle Paul makes the same point: 'For you know the grace of our Lord Jesus Christ, that though he was rich, yet for your sakes he became poor, so that you through his poverty might become rich' (2 Corinthians 8:9).

The journey for Jesus to Bethlehem was a journey of love, sacrifice and total self-giving. He made it for us.

A prayer:
Lord, help my life reflect that I accept I was the purpose of your journey.

No Recognition

••

'He was in the world, and though the world was made through him,
the world did not recognise him' (v. 10).

Unless something is badly wrong in relationships, home is where we are always welcome. It's where we are known and accepted for who we are. It's where we belong. In this regard, today's verses pose a few questions. When God came to earth in Christ he was, in effect, coming home. He had made the world, he owned the world and he belonged in his world (Matthew 21:37). But he wasn't recognised. And the more he revealed his true nature and identity, the less welcome he became. All this suggests that the people in the world had grown away from their Creator. Although made in his image (Genesis 1:26), their image of him had changed or become distorted.

We recognise people in a variety of ways – by their faces, their voices, their handwriting, the way they walk, sometimes by their dress, or even smell! We also recognise people by their actions and reactions, by their attitudes and values. We come to expect the people we know to act in certain ways – even if we expect some of them to be unpredictable!

How should Jesus have been recognised and how do we recognise his presence today? Should the people of his day have been drawn to him, captivated by his goodness and integrity? Should they have identified his humility and obedience to his Father as real evidence of his divinity – qualities to be embraced and emulated? Well, they didn't – and by all the evidence, our generation doesn't do any better. There is little or no recognition of any need to recognise him.

Jesus encourages us today to see him in each other (Matthew 25:40). He also gives his Spirit to those who invite him into the centre of their lives. He is recognisable in those who do so, in natural and confirming ways.

••

To ponder:
How easily or readily do I look for Christ in the people I meet?

With Us

....

'The Word became flesh and made his dwelling among us' (v. 14).

There are different ways in which we can be 'with' other people. We can be with them in the physical sense of being in the group. We can be with them by being on their side in a dispute or a game. We can be with others 'in spirit', when we can't be with them in a certain place at a certain time. We can also be with friends in sympathy and encouragement – or simply by living with them.

When Jesus 'made his dwelling among us' (v. 14), God had arrived physically. John's first letter expands this point: 'That which was from the beginning, which we have heard, which we have seen with our eyes, which we have looked at and our hands have touched – this we proclaim concerning the Word of life' (1 John 1:1). God in Christ was with us. He was real and he was here.

He was also with us in the sense of being on our side. In spite of our reluctance to welcome him, he hadn't come to condemn us but to save us (John 3:17). Although we had been unwilling to identify with him, he was identifying with us – in every human way. John tells us he 'became flesh' with all the senses, deprivations and challenges that come with it.

Yet intrinsic to this identification is his loyalty to us when we most need him. He stays with us when others might walk away or keep a distance. When we have disgraced ourselves and the shame is overpowering, he is still there – with us. When it seems we have nothing to offer and all our resources are spent, he doesn't abandon us.

If we can grasp the far-reaching implications of 'Immanuel . . . God with us' (Matthew 1:23), Jesus' journey to Bethlehem will again have had its desired effect.

....

> The Word is spoken as a baby cries,
> Heaven with earth identifies,
> God among us, lives and dies,
> Immanuel.

R. S.

The One and Only

....

'For God so loved the world that he gave his one and only Son, that whoever believes in him shall not perish but have eternal life' (v. 16).

It isn't possible to relate fully God the Father's relationship with his Son to our family relationships with each other, but there's no doubt the New Testament writers want us to understand the cost involved in Jesus coming to earth. John tells us that God gave his one and only Son (v. 16). He also uses the term 'One and Only' as a title for Jesus in the introduction to his Gospel (1:14). There is something precious about a 'one and only', as well as something distinct and unique. We are right to think of Jesus in each of these terms.

Expanding on the theme, John uses a further two words to illustrate the distinctive nature of Jesus – 'full of grace and truth' (1:14). No one else has ever measured up to this standard.

In Western countries we speak of a father 'giving away' his daughter in a wedding ceremony. In effect the daughter moves into the care of her husband. Within mutual, loving relationship, responsibility is 'transferred'. My wife and I have a 'one and only' daughter and some years ago I 'gave her away' to Matthew in confidence and thanksgiving. It was a happy, warm occasion.

When God gave his one and only Son to us, he placed the infant Jesus in the care of Mary and Joseph. Much as they loved him, God the Father was aware that the world into which his Son had been placed wouldn't be so kind. There was no confidence in Jesus being safe from harm – quite the reverse.

The cost of the giving away at Bethlehem is beyond words (2 Corinthians 9:15).

....

To ponder:
If Jesus was described as full of 'grace and truth', which two words would others use to apply to me?

Bethlehem's Wake-up Call

....

'An angel of the Lord appeared in a dream to Joseph in Egypt and said, "Get up, take the child and his mother and go to the land of Israel, for those who were trying to take the child's life are dead"'
(vv. 19, 20).

The Joseph of Genesis was known as a dreamer (ch. 37). The Joseph charged with being a father to Jesus also had dreams. We are told of two in Matthew's birth narrative – both far-reaching in their implications. This dream prompted Joseph to action. He moved from hiding in Egypt – and on to the rest of his life with Mary and Jesus.

When Phillips Brooks wrote about Bethlehem, following a visit to the town, he suggested it was dreamless. His carol sees Bethlehem as not noticing the 'everlasting' significance of what was happening right under the noses of its inhabitants:

> O little town of Bethlehem,
> How still we see thee lie!
> Above thy deep and dreamless sleep
> The silent stars go by.
> Yet in thy dark streets shineth
> The everlasting light;
> The hopes and fears of all the years
> Are met in thee tonight.

A 'deep and dreamless' sleep could be an apt description of our world this Christmas. It has forgotten to expect anything from God. It doesn't usually notice when he is doing a great thing – because it isn't interested. We need the kind of wake-up call Phillips Brooks gave.

....

To ponder:
'We never become truly spiritual by sitting down and wishing to become so. You must undertake something so great that you cannot accomplish it unaided.'

Phillips Brooks

Christmas Child

....

'The child's father and mother were full of wonder at what was being said about him' (v. 33, NEB).

We believe that in the person of Jesus Christ the divine and human natures are united, so that he is truly and properly God and truly and properly human.

Christ Came

Christ came!
A lad like any other.
The 'boy next door',
Your own kid-brother.
Yes, Glory 'In Excelsis Deo'
But rather like
Our grandson Theo!
The Child of Man, and Child of God,
Armed with a home-made
Fishing rod!
He came from heaven's
Other skies,
With mortal mischief
In his eyes.
But in his boyish face
We saw
Fresh beauty,
Never guessed before;
God's power, his peace,
His love, his joy,
All poured into
One little boy.
He came!
The whole wide world
To bless;
Our Father, Spirit, Son,
No less!

They Bowed Down

....

*'On coming to the house, they saw the child with his mother Mary,
and they bowed down and worshipped him' (v. 11).*

I have visited Bethlehem four times and have entered the Nativity
Church on each occasion. The church isn't among the grandest and
most impressive in the world – and perhaps that is in keeping with the
belief that it is built over the cave in which the Son of God came into
the world. The entrance isn't very impressive either. The door is quite
small, and low. In fact, unless you are a small child you are certain to
need to stoop to enter. We are told this design was intended – that all
who come to worship the Christ-child must first of all bow. In so doing,
pilgrims are following in good footsteps.

> Once I saw a king bow down,
> Lay before the child a crown.

I understand that the carol from which these words are taken was
written by D. Weekes.[3] Helped by music from Terry Camsey, I picture
these words coming from a seven- or eight-year-old girl, peering
through the stable door with wonder written all over her face. 'What is
going on?' she is asking herself. This is a king – with all his regalia –
bowing down to a baby. And then . . . off comes his crown and with
grace, dignity and subjection he lays it down. It is an act of total
surrender to the King of Kings. It is our privilege to do the same.

The God who has laid himself bare of everything – for us – more than
merits our homage. We live in an age when we recognise that we can
talk with God in any place, at any time and in any situation. But
shouldn't there be times when we are simply compelled to bow in
worship?

....

To ponder:
**Why does this generation find it so difficult to kneel and bow
down to its Maker?**

Not Very Far

....

*'Come, let us bow down in worship, let us kneel before
the LORD our Maker' (v. 6).*

To arrive in the small room under the Nativity Church where it is
believed Jesus was born requires some kind of response. To simply
listen to the guide, express thanks and leave is to act like a tourist and
not a pilgrim. Groups I have been with have wanted to share a Bible
reading and, if possible, a song – especially 'O come let us adore him,
Christ the Lord!' Prayers have followed. Private prayers, personal
prayers, shared prayers.

The stable or cave in which Jesus was born marked a new beginning
for humankind. It marks a new beginning for many who find that the
Lord is still there. Whatever prayers are made when we finally arrive
at Bethlehem in spirit, they cannot simply be left there. If they are
meant, if the adoration and gratitude we express are sincere, they will
affect the way we live.

In Old Testament times worship was linked to service. The worship
of God and the service of God meant practically the same thing. It is a
theme developed in the New Testament. Writing to the Romans, Paul
says: 'Offer your bodies as living sacrifices, holy and pleasing to God –
this is your spiritual act of worship' (12:1). We worship God by the way
we live.

Worship and service aren't always linked today. 'Corporate worship'
– offered to God in a church setting for instance – can at times seem
divorced from the realities of life. It can become something we 'do' –
as if God was the audience! Worship which expects no response is
something we might give to a baby, the Christ-child, but not to our
Saviour and Lord. Worship shouldn't be isolated from our normal life.
It is about relationship – a deep meeting with God that involves
interaction, and includes being open to his will at all times.

Bethlehem reminds us that God is always moving towards us. How
far is it to Bethlehem? God's continuing initiative shows us it needn't
be very far at all.

Regrets

Introduction

We all know what it is to be sorry for something we have done, or failed to do. Sometimes it is almost a trifling matter in the great scheme of things – a forgotten birthday, an overlooked anniversary. Sometimes it is a lingering regret for something we said, or forgot to say. And sometimes it is a deep sense of shame we just can't shake off.

Whatever, all regret is best acknowledged, not least to ourselves – and when reparation or restitution can be made, we should not delay. Wounds are better healed. The Bible has something to say about this, as we shall discover in these last few days of the year.

> I wasted it!
> It's gone,
> And I repent.
> The precious day
> You gave me
> Came and went!
> It wasn't really mine
> To throw away.
> I'm sorry that I
> Used it up that way.
>
> Remind me
> That my days are just
> On loan.
> Forgive me
> When I treat them
> As my own.
> But here's another,
> Fresh and clean
> And new.
> Help me to use it
> Wisely, Lord,
> For you!

You Are the Man!

••

'David burned with anger against the man and said to Nathan,
"As surely as the Lord lives, the man who did this deserves to die . . .
because he did such a thing and had no pity." Then Nathan
said to David, "You are the man!"' (vv. 5–7).

The end of the year is an appropriate time for us to examine our mistakes and express our regrets. Some sincere tears might not go amiss. Those who say 'sorry' and those who hear those words addressed to them will be the better for the exchange.

The renowned French singer Edith Piaf shared her philosophy about regret in song: 'No regrets! I regret nothing!' she declared. Did she mean it? I would be surprised if she did. Her tumultuous life gave her much to look back on with sorrow, and she clearly nursed many emotional wounds.

King David's thinking was very different. When faced with his weaknesses and sins he admitted them immediately and repented of them. Just as an infected wound can pass on infection, unconfessed sin can harm our relationships with other people. Another singer says: 'You always hurt the one you love, the one you shouldn't hurt at all.' The unconfessed and the unregretted are both dangerous.

David's public expression of repentance was a healthy thing. It is recorded for us, as swiftly as David said to Nathan: '"I have sinned against the Lord", Nathan replied: "The Lord has taken away your sin"' (v. 13). We must not pretend that sin can be easily dismissed. But we are all sinners and we should acknowledge that through genuine regret and changed behaviour.

While it can be a good thing to be our own accuser it is not for us to decide our own punishment, although our remorse can be painful. May we so live in 2008 that we have less to regret this time next year!

....

To ponder:
'If we hold on to our mistake we can't see our own glory in the mirror because we have the mistake between our face and the mirror, so we can't see what we are capable of being.'

Maya Angelou

Visible Regret

*'Peter was hurt because Jesus asked him the third time,
"Do you love me?" He said, "Lord, you know all things;
you know that I love you" (v. 17).*

Peter did not receive any pieces of silver in return for his words, but when he denied knowing Jesus he betrayed his Master as surely as Judas Iscariot did. We are told that after Peter uttered his words of denial, the Lord turned and looked upon him . . . and the look caused Peter to go out and weep bitterly.

How he must have regretted his actions! What shame he must have felt when the cock crowed, and many times thereafter. Have I ever felt such shame? Oh, yes – most often through thoughtless actions which have denied my discipleship.

Peter was hurt again when it seemed that Jesus did not accept his post-resurrection protestations of love. Twice was doubly painful. Three times was unbearable. But then he heard Jesus utter words that put everything right: 'You still have a job with me. It's the same job as mine. Be a good shepherd. Care for my sheep. You're needed!' (my paraphrase). Peter must have sensed he was being forgiven.

Forgiven! Is there a more glorious word, a more wonderful experience? Henry Ward Beecher declared: 'Repentance is another name for aspiration' and Reinhold Niebuhr wrote: 'We are saved by hope.' Aspiration, hope – good words to consider as a new year approaches.

Perhaps the current year hasn't been a glorious one. Perhaps, like Peter, we look back on things of which we are less than proud. But there is a new year before us and we are still employed in God's service. Who cares where or how!

And still there are fields where the labourers are few,
And still there are souls without bread,
And still eyes that weep where the darkness is deep,
And still straying sheep to be led.

Albert Orsborn

Not Disobedient

••

'"I was not disobedient to the vision from heaven. First to those in Damascus, then to those in Jerusalem and in all Judea, and to the Gentiles also, I preached that they should repent and turn to God and prove their repentance by their deeds" (vv. 19, 20).

No one turned the world upside down more thoroughly than Paul, but first his own world had to be overturned by Christ. Paul's activities take our breath away. Once a dedicated enemy of the Christians, he became their best missionary. Educated and sophisticated though he was, he was at home with the most ordinary of people as well as the most polished. When funds were low he could put his hand to tent-making, but when he had to drop his tools to chat with King Agrippa about spiritual things that was all right by him. It was part of his ministry.

Paul never regretted his calling, even though it required him to experience practically everything most of us would evade at any price. When Paul said 'yes' to the call of Christ he could have had little idea of what he would face. To read the account of his travels makes me wish I was a Hollywood film producer with a bottomless budget!

Paul was imprisoned many times, flogged, stoned, and shipwrecked three times. We can read all about it in 2 Corinthians 11:16-33. He never gave up, never caved in and – as today's reading reminds us – was never disobedient to the guidance of the Holy Spirit.

We should all be motivated to better things by Paul's testimony: 'I make myself a slave to everyone, to win as many as possible' (1 Corinthians 9:19). If only more of us had Paul's ability and willingness to try anything for the sake of the gospel! We would surely reach the ending of each year with fewer regrets about missed opportunities to witness for our Lord. Do I feel a new year resolution coming on?

••

To ponder:
How would I cope if my world was turned upside down by the Holy Spirit? Do I have the spiritual stability to remain upright?

Regret Can Turn to Joy

....

'Joseph said to them: "Don't be afraid. Am I in the place of God? You intended to harm me, but God intended it for good to accomplish what is now being done, the saving of many lives"' (vv. 19, 20).

Samuel Logan Brengle was an outstanding writer of books about holiness – an accomplishment which came about through very negative circumstances. He had long been a noted teacher and preacher on the subject but wrote little on it until he was hospitalised after being struck by a brick thrown during an early-day Salvation Army open-air meeting he was taking part in. Frustrated at not being able to preach, Brengle took up the suggestion of a friend that he should write. A new ministry emerged which he maintained for the rest of his life.

Brengle had a sense of humour and kept the brick, on which he had inscribed the *King James Version* of Joseph's words: 'As for you, ye thought evil against me; but God meant it unto good.' John Newton had a similar near-death experience prior to becoming a Christian, and also kept a copy of those words on his mantelpiece. We could remind ourselves of that when we sing his hymn, 'Amazing Grace'.

We should not be too quick to regret the negative things which happen to us. Our Father in heaven can turn them to good. Many of us can recall sad or difficult times which turned out to be purposeful and sometimes even joyful! I was not happy when my one-year spell at the Salvation Army's officer-training college was extended to two – but those circumstances led me to fall in love with a French officer-cadet in the same situation. We have now been married for fifty years. Joy indeed!

Don't write things off too soon. The sadnesses and worries of 2007 could yet become things of beauty and a joy forever!

....

O Joy that seekest me through pain,
I cannot close my heart to thee;
I trace the rainbow through the rain
And feel the promise is not vain,
That morn shall tearless be.
George Matheson

Christmas Surprise

....

'The Word became flesh; he came to dwell among us' (v. 14, NEB).

Let it never be taken for granted that Christ wore flesh and blood in order that our spiritual growth might be real and beautiful. God save us from becoming accustomed to its meaning and majesty!

Surprise! Surprise!

I don't quite know what I should say
As I kneel down upon the hay;
It clothes the floor but rubs my knees –
Would someone like to help me, please?
I came to say hello to God,
So took the trail the wise men trod.
They seemed to think they knew the way,
And I'd prepared some things to say.
But now I'm taken by surprise,
In fact I can't believe my eyes:
To think that folk make such a fuss
For one who looks so much like us!
Two hands, two feet, two eyes, one nose . . .
But someone special, I suppose.
Has somehow slipped inside the wrappings?
How else explain the angel trappings?
Is God himself inside this Child?
Can God Almighty be so mild?
I do believe the Baby smiled!

What a Waste!

· ·

'Jesus said again, "Children, how hard it is to enter the kingdom of God! It is easier for a camel to go through the eye of a needle than for a rich man to enter the kingdom of God"' (vv. 24, 25).

Matthew, Mark and Luke sometimes tell the same story in very similar ways, but occasionally one adds something unique. For example, Mark 10:21 tells us: 'Jesus looked at him and loved him.' Jesus was impressed by this man, saw in him the kind of disciple he needed. All three Synoptic Gospel writers agree that the man was rich, and two share the fact that he was young, but only Luke tells us the man fell on his knees. All say that after Jesus spoke the man left, but only Mark tells us 'the man's face fell' (v. 22). So, two people regretted the outcome of the discussion: Jesus and the man we have come to know as the rich young ruler.

Jesus could not have the young man on his team while he held on to the false security of his money, and the candidate wouldn't come without it. What a pity! Jesus lost a potentially good disciple. The young man lost more than he would ever realise. However, had he followed Jesus but held on to his wealth it would always have been an obstacle. The Master who was prepared to have nowhere to lay his head could not be served by a disciple always looking for a five-star hotel.

There are plenty of rich candidates for discipleship these days: men and women with a wealth of education, creativity, experience in business; people with rich personalities and gifts of leadership. Many are admired by the world and appreciated by those who work with or for them. But sometimes that 'wealth' gets in the way. Jesus looks at them and loves them, but wants them for what they are, not what they have. And some find it impossible to let go.

Such 'rich young rulers' surely regret their decisions in later life when they realise they might have been a Peter, a Thomas, a Luke or a Paul. May they, every 31 December, realise the possibilities of 1 January: 'A star is there that once is seen, you may always be what you might have been.' It's the Gospel of the Second Chance.

Notes

1. William Neil, *William Neil's One Volume Bible Commentary*, 1962, Hodder & Stoughton.
2. Harry Blamires, *A God Who Acts*, 1983, SPCK.
3. D. Weekes, *A Christmas Lullaby*, 1957, SP&S Ltd.

INDEX
September–December 2007
(as from May–August 2002)

....